A complete guide to the three great cities of the
Ancient ANTALYA - Pamphylia
PERGE
ASPENDOS
SİDE

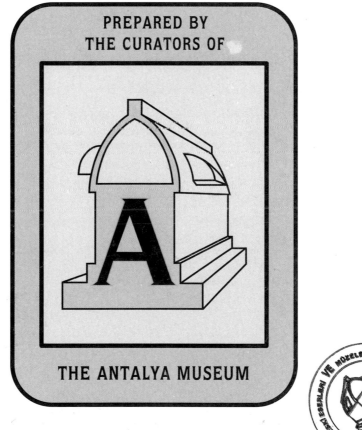

PREPARED BY
THE CURATORS OF

THE ANTALYA MUSEUM

ISBN 975-17-1731-0

Antalya Museum Publication III
April 1997

THIS GUIDE BOOK HAS COMPLIED FOR THE MUSEUM
UNDER THE CONTRIBUTION OF THE MUSEUM DIRECTOR

Metin PEHLİVANER

AND MUSEUM CURATORS

İ. Akan ATİLA - Orhan ATVUR - Sabri AYDAL - Ferhan BÜYÜKYÖRÜK - Ünal ÇINAR
Nermin ÇOLAK - Mustafa DEMİREL - Ünal DEMİRER - Mehmet ERDEM
Hamdi KODAN - Selahattin KOR - Edip ÖZGÜR - Cihan TİBET - Ahmet TOPBAŞ
İlhan ÜNLÜSOY - Azize YENER

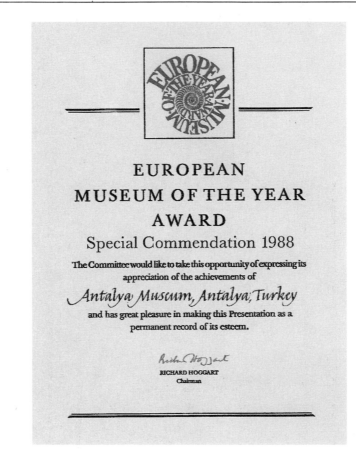

EUROPEAN
MUSEUM OF THE YEAR
AWARD
Special Commendation 1988

The Committee would like to take this opportunity of expressing its
appreciation of the achievements of

Antalya Museum, Antalya, Turkey

and has great pleasure in making this Presentation as a
permanent record of its esteem.

RICHARD HOGGART
Chairman

- Revised and Edited by   : İ. Akan ATİLA - M. Edip ÖZGÜR
- Translation by   : Niğar ALEMDAR - Dr .Üner BEKÖZ - Meral CAN
- Photography by   : İ.A. ATİLA, O. ATVUR, T. BİRGİLİ, Ü. ÇINAR, Güney Kartpostal ve Turistik Yayıncılık, Esin ÖZGÜR
- Printed by   : DÖNMEZ OFFSET - MüZE ESERLERİ TURİSTİK YAYINLARI - ANKARA
                             G.M.K. Bl. 77/E - 06570 Maltepe - Ankara • (312) 229 7961 - (312) 229 2569

Dedicated to Prof. Dr. Jale İNAN.

CONTENTS

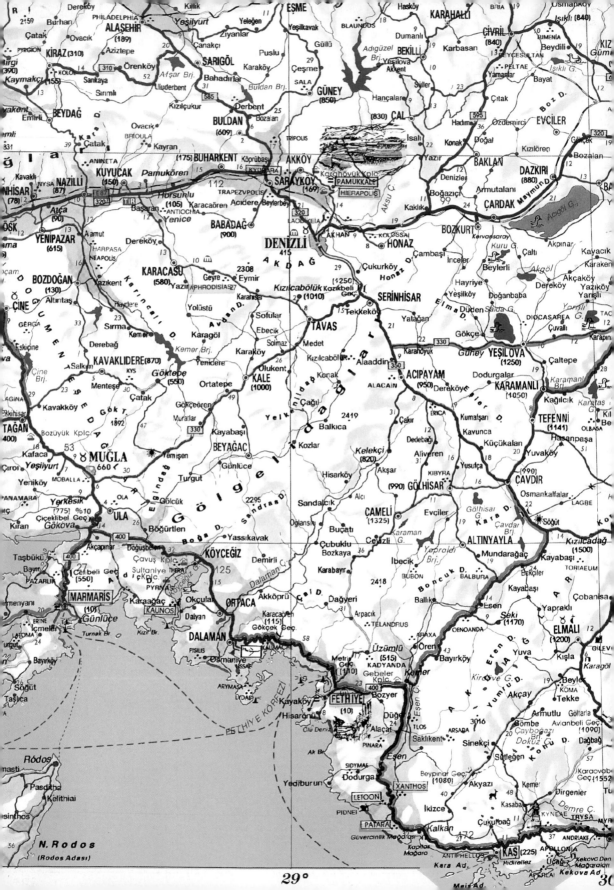

CHRONOLOGY OF PAMPHYLIA

Palaeolithic Period ⇨ 8000 B.C.

Neolithic Period ⇨ 8000-5500 B.C.

Chalcolithic Period ⇨ 5500-3000 B.C.

Early Bronze Ages ⇨ 3000-2000 B.C..

Middle - Late Bronze Ages ⇨ 2000-1200 B.C.

New Hittite Kingdoms ⇨ 1200-700 B.C.

Urartian Kingdom ⇨ 900-600 B.C.

Phrygian Kingdom ⇨ 700-550 B.C.

Lydian Kingdom ⇨ 700-550 B.C.

Hellenistic Period ⇨ 330-30 B.C.

Roman Period ⇨ 30 B.C.-330 A.D

Early Christian/Byzantine Period ⇨ 330-1453 A.D.

Seljuk Period ⇨ 1071-1300 A.D.

Ottoman Period ⇨ 1299-1923 (Proclamation of the Turkish Republic)

INTRODUCTION

LAND AND HISTORY

The province of Antalya lies along the Southern Mediterranean shores of Turkey, shaped like a crescent, about 300 miles in length, separated from the mainland by the Taurus Mountains. The Taurus Range, that reach to peaks nearly nine thousand feet, and come down to the sea carrying along pine forests, rivers, and forming charming bays, beaches and dramatic cascades falling from cliffs, provide this region with cool and breezy platos and thus transform Antalya's climate into an eternal spring all the year around. So during the same day, it becomes possible to ski in the mountains, and then enjoy the very fine sand beaches along the shores. Swimming season starts early in April and ends in late October. Besides this wonderful climate which makes Antalya the loveliest resort place of the whole Mediterranean, she has more to offer to the tourists since the beginnings of history, many civilizations have flourished in this area.

In Antalya the modern times mingle with the ancient; every corner of the region offers something no other possibly can: it is the two hundred thousand years of human history which began by the hand of Neanderthal man of various cultures and civilizations, and every side track brings the tourist into the extacy of exploring into the mystical ancient. There are more than ninety historical sites many of which are still in excellent condition and fairly accessible.

Antalya and its vicinity has been inhabited since the prehistoric times. Excavations conducted at "Karain Cave" and its vicinity, near the village of Yağca, 25 km North-West of Antalya have provided us with findings from periods as early as the Palaeolithic period. It is now suggested, depending on the latest data, that the first man-made stone tools found in Karain demonstrate a special technology- to be named "Karainstone technology-" - dating back 200,000 years, and more, the suggestion that the time might go farther is to come forward. This is high time we reminded that not alone for the world in Anatolia but for all Mediterranean, that was the revolution of man-kind, thinking "Neanderthal Men" besides the stone. In the same cave are the messengers of the mankind to leap into age of agriculture, of the revolution of Neanderthal men an exceptional corner in the history; painted pottery samples, carbonized figs and wheat. These finds are similar to those of central Anatolian settlements of the same age. The Antalya region has had links with the Western lake districts and the central Anatolian cultures via the Westward Çubuk and Yenice passes ever since then.

It is not known today how the Antalya region passed from prehistoric to the historical periods. We know that the Hittites who settled mainly in the great loop of the Halys River, extended their borders across Asia Minor. Written Hittite documents of the end of the 2 nd millennium B.C. make mention of "Achiyawa" or "Arzawa" land, which is supposed to be in the Antalya region. However, no finds have been made as yet to verify this supposition.

We know that the Achaeans had developed a highly cultured civilisation as "The Minoan Civilisation" in the Crete island. Their expansion towards East (1400-1300 B.C.) included the Aegean Islands, Rhodes, Cyprus and Antalya region too, between 1300-1200 B.C. Although Mycenaean finds are quite numerous in West and SouthWest Anatolia, none have been discovered as yet in Antalya region. It is probable, as the great writers of antiquity accept, that

- Red Figured Column Krater (Tibet Krater)
- Found in 1991, from the Classical Necropolis of Karaçallı
- Classical Period, end of 5th or begining of 4th century B.C. - Antalya Museum

   Red-figured column-krater decorated two metops on the body. One of which is decorated with four, while other with three youths having fun and drinking. Each picture field bordered above by a kymation.

Achaeans did land in region. This is only verified so far by linguistic similarities. The modern province of Antalya consists of the following regions in the historical periods: Pamphylia entirely, Cilicia, Pisidia and Lycia in parts.

The region called "Pamphylia" which means "land of all tribes" is located on the central part of Antalya province and it encompasses the whole of present day plain. The land originated in the Post-Miocene period, today it is an alluvial plain formed by the rivers of the region. The climate here is well adapted for survival and for all kinds of vegetation. The land descends in stages towards the sea from the Taurus Mountains. Since the earliest times the settlement and survival had been easy,because of the fertility of the soil and the natural irrigation of the land by the rivers Catarhactes (Düden), Cestros (Aksu), Eurymedon (Köprüçay), and Melas (Manavgat).

From after the Trojan war (13 th Century B.C.) to the 7 th Century B.C. Pamphylia was reinhabited by the tribes from Greece, by the Ionians and Aeolians. The cities of Perge, Aspendos and Side were included in this new immigrations. Since these city names are of Anatolian origin, and not Greek, the newcomers must not have made new settlements but simply invaded the area and occupied existing sites.

Pamphylia never attained political autonomy; but was always under the control of the Anatolian States or of the power which ruled the whole of Anatolia. After this colonization there is a gap in Pamphylian history until the time of Lydian rule. According to Herodotus; Croesus, the Lydian king, invaded Pamphylia too, in 547-546 B.C.

After the Lydian kingdom had been brought to an end by the Persians, Pamphylia came under Persian rule and was included in the first satrapy, which was a governmental unit of the Persian Empire. Some cities continued minting their own coinage, showing that Persian rule had some tolerance in government.

Persian control continued until Alexander the Great invaded Pamphylia (334 B.C.) After his death, the empire was divided among his generals. Antigonos was the first, but he lost his lands at the battle of Ipsos (301 B.C.) and the new ruler was Pleistarkos, the brother of Cassender, the king of Macedonia. After his fall, Pamphylia was governed sometimes by the Ptolemies, who tried to gain over the Eastern Mediterranean, and sometimes by the Seleucids in Syria. When the Syrian king Antiochus III was defeated in the Battle of Magnesia (190 B.C.) that put an end to Seleucid rule in Asia Minor. The Roman general Manlius conquered Pamphylia and imposed tribute on. We do not know if the Pamphylian region was handed over to Pergamon at the Peace Treaty of Apamea (188 B.C.) But quite soon afterwards the Western part of Pamphylia was invaded by the Pergamene king Attalos II, it was at that time the port-city of Attaleia was founded.

In 133 B.C. Pamphylia was bequeathed to the Romans in the will of Attalos III, the last Pergemene king. After a period of freedom, it formed part of the province of Cilicia that was annexed by Rome in 103 B.C.

In 36 B.C. it was given to the Galatian king Amyntas by Mark Antony who ruled the Eastern part of Roman Empire. After Amyntas' death (25 B.C.), Galatia was made into a Roman province, and Pamphylia was again joined to Cilicia. In A.D. 43 the emperor Claudius combined Lycia and Pamphylia into a Roman province and it continued as such until the middle of the 4 th cent. A.D.

1-2 Cotton and Orange from
    Pamphylia plain.

3   Konyaaltı Beach

4   Ski center of Saklıkent

1 Black Cave - Oldest settlement of the Antalya region.

2 Chipped flint-stone tools. Middle Palaeolithic Period (Mousterian type) from the Black Cave

3 Recent excavation in Black Cave

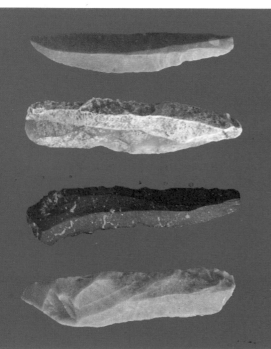

The Karain Cave near Village of Yağca and 30 km. North-West of Antalya. The Cave was first excavated by Prof. İ.Kılıç Kökten from the University of Ankara in 1946. Only a portion of the fifty-meter cave has been explored so far. The cave consists of three large inter-connected spaces where finds from the Palaeolithic, the Mesolithic, the Chalcolithic, Bronze and later ages were discovered under 10,5 meters thick deposits.

Paulus had visited Pamphylia many times within his mission travels to plant the religion, the same time Emperor Claudius governed. Paulus established Christian multitudes, organised the network between them and protected the pureness of the basics by sending notifications. The true settler of the Christian church organisation is Paulus himself. That is why we are to accept that there happened a Christian organisation in Pamphylia since then although it needed a certainly long time for the Christianity to root and play effective roles.

Pamphylia attained its richest and most prosperous period in the 2 nd and 3 rd centuries A.D. Its wealth grew as her cities expanded. New monumental buildings were erected by rich citizens. In the 5 th cent. A.D. Christianity began to appear in Pamphylia. Side and Perge became two important centres of Christendom. By the Byzantine period, Pamphylia was again a province. In the 8 th and 9 th centuries A.D. it suffered Arabic attacks and was conquered by the Seljuk Sultan Gıyaseddin Keyhüsrev I.

After the fall of the Konya Seljuk State in 1299, she joined "the Tekelioğulları" (Tekeli-sons sovereignty) which is a branch of "the Hamitoğulları", the local provincial rulers of Pamphylia, and in the time of Sultan Murat I (1391 A.D.) it came under Ottoman domination. It has ever since been an integral part of the Ottoman Empire and, since 1923 of the Republic of Turkey.

Regarding the above information, Pamphylia's naval strategy, between Lycia and Cilicia where is now East of province of Antalya in the South shore of Anatolia, right in front of the Taurus Mountains, withdrawing Northward, has now become more enlightened.

Sovereignty of the seas means the sovereignty of the sea routes and sovereignty of the routes means having the main transportation vessels run or interrupt. When a power controls the navigation of the boats on the water in a particular region, it means that he sovereigns the water. In case this sovereignty covers an area whose borders become away from mother land, the power then needs bases abroad.

That was why Athens in 5 th cent B.C. had held the sovereignty of the surrounding waters as she invaded some islands and shores of the Aegean Sea. Similarly, Ptolemaios in Egypt in 3 rd cent. B.C. governed Phonikos, Cyprus, Pamphylia, Crete and many other islands in the Aegean Sea as well as some of the cities in the West bank of Anatolia and proved its sovereignty in these waters.

Eastern Mediterranean Sea is a closed water which then and today has been a strategically whole for the coasting countries to sovereign. The sovereignty, however, might become possible by only the invasion and/or governing the major naval bases such as Phonikos, Cyprus, month of River Nile and Pamphylia.

For a state, having the sovereignty this part of the Mediterranean Sea, Pamphylia was the farthest extremity of the naval bases system.

Never had Pamphylia played a major role in political arena and always been depended to other states. Three major cities of the region; Perge, Aspendos and Side had never trusted one another and survival as autonomic societies of Greek polices. The population earned living by agriculture, fishery and especially marine trade.

Finally, while Pamphylia had never independently taken and important part in political area, it had always been regarded with envious eyes for it was in the very point of naval trade lines.

🔖 Waterfall of Kurşunlu

Photo : Don Frey

The commercial amphoras of the Eastern Mediterranean Region.

PERGE

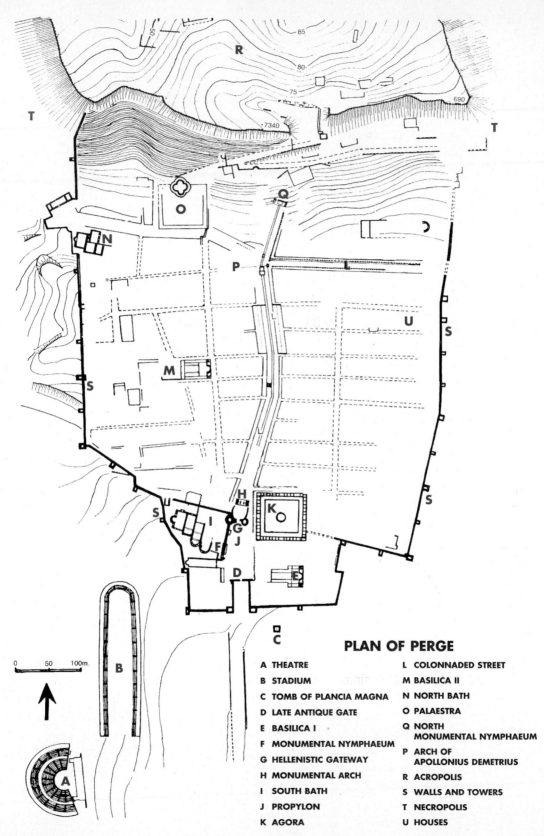

PLAN OF PERGE

A THEATRE
B STADIUM
C TOMB OF PLANCIA MAGNA
D LATE ANTIQUE GATE
E BASILICA I
F MONUMENTAL NYMPHAEUM
G HELLENISTIC GATEWAY
H MONUMENTAL ARCH
I SOUTH BATH
J PROPYLON
K AGORA

L COLONNADED STREET
M BASILICA II
N NORTH BATH
O PALAESTRA
Q NORTH
   MONUMENTAL NYMPHAEUM
P ARCH OF
   APOLLONIUS DEMETRIUS
R ACROPOLIS
S WALLS AND TOWERS
T NECROPOLIS
U HOUSES

0   50   100m.

THE HISTORY OF PERGE

Ancient city of Perge, the nearest archeological site to the city of Antalya, is located 2 km. North of the Aksu subdistrict and 17 km. from Antalya on the Antalya-Alanya highway. Perge was founded approximately in the center of the Pamphylia plains-probably the most suitable location in the area. Although about 12 km. inland, Perge maintained an outlet to the Mediterranean Sea via the Aksu River (the ancient Cestros), 4 km to its East. The site chosen for the city not only provided protection from attacks from the sea but also enabled the partial employment of ancient city planning. The city was first established on a 60 m. elevation with a flat top but with steep sides. The acropolis was situated on this hill on the North. To the South-East of the remains of the acropolis, there is the İyilikbelen Hill. To the South-West, there is the Kocabelen Hill on which the theater leans. In the Hellenistic Period (300-200 B.C.) Perge developed between these three elevations; in the Roman Period (200-300 A.D.), however, the city grew beyond this nucleus.

The two main avenues with water canals running in the middle, form a T-shape in front of the acropolis as well as the major lines of the city plan. The side streets opening perpendicularly onto these main avenues at equal intervals, show partial application of Hippodomian planning.

Writers such as Scylax (4 th century B.C.), Pliny (1 st century B.C.), Strabo (1 st cent. A.D.) and Ptolemaios (2 nd cent. A.D.) refer to Perge as the most important city of Pamphylia.

Located on the ancient route that started in Pergamon and ended in Side, Perge owed this importance especially to the Aksu (Cestros) River, one of the two major rivers that irrigate the Pamphylian plains. The Cestros emerges from the Pisidia Mountains in the North. Today it is known as the Kocaçay in the Taurus Mountains and as the Aksu River in the Pamphylia plains. Although the river is no longer suited for transport, in antiquity it not only made the land fertile, but also played a very important role in providing transportation for Perge. The ancient writer Strabo records that Perge was 60 stadia (12 km.) inland on the river Cestros, while Pomponius Mela writes that the river was very suitable for transportation. Moreover, in the Acts of the Apostles in the Bible, St.Paul and his friends are reported to have sailed from Paphos in Cyprus to Perge. No doubt, such a journey could only have been realized via the Cestros river. The impact of this river on the city can be traced throughout the history of Perge on coins, on reliefs, and in the statue of the river god Cestros, found at the Monumental Nymphaeum on the southern slope of the acropolis.

The fate of Perge, one of the oldest towns of the Pamphylia region, has been closely linked with the history of the area, because Pamphylia's strategically important location on the Mediterranean coast has constantly attracted the attention of her neighbors.

According to the results of archeological excavations and research conducted to this day, one can say the city of Perge definitely enjoyed three glorious periods in history. The first of these periods is the Hellenistic period (the third and second centuries B.C.) represented by the magnificient city walls and towers which are still partially erect. Much like many other Anatolian cities, the second glorious period of Perge corresponds with the Roman period, that is the second and third centuries A.D. Many monumental buildings such as the theater, the stadium, the baths, the nymphaeums, and the agora, most of which are erect today, are works that depict that period. Perge's last period of affluence coincides with the Christian Period- the fifth and sixth centuries A.D. In this period, Perge became the seat of a metropolitan (archbishop) and many churches were constructed.

SITE PLAN OF PERGE

A Theatre
  Theater

B Stadium
  Stadion

C City Gate
  Tor

D Hellenistic Gate
  Hellenistisch pforte

E Agora
  Markt

F Nymphaeum
  Nympheum

G Church
  Kirchen

H Propylaeum
  Propylaeum

I Baths
  Thermen

J Colonnaded street
  Hallenstrassen

K Basilica
  Basilika

L Acropolis
  Akropolis

M Fortifications
  Befestigungsmauer

N Palaestra
  Palast

by ALFRED W. HARRIS
JANE HANSON HARRIS

A General view of Perge from the İyilikbelen Hill.

Aside from some philological clues and hypotheses, there is no concrete information on the pre-historic periods of Perge. However, if one considers the fact that the Luvian language used in Asia Minor circa 3000 B.C. mentions Pamphylia, one can then conclude that the city of Perge was inhabited as early as 3000 B.C. The latest evidence supporting this theory is a bronze tablet unearthed in the Hittite capital Hatushash (Boğazköy) where Perge is a mentioned. This view is also supported by the name "Perge" which has no linguistic connection with ancient Greek. "Perge" is undoubtedly an old Anatolian name. Similarly Artemis Pergaia, the foremost goddess of the city, is not a Greek goddess but a nature goddess whose cult goes back to very early periods in Anatolia. The name of this goddess depicted on Perge coins and votive inscriptions, is written as "WANESSA PREIIA" (queen of Perge) in the local Pamphylian vernacular, in keeping with the old traditions and thus attesting to the age of the city.

The Achaean colonization in Pamphylia (2000 B.C.) is also verified by the abundance of the Arcadian linguistic elements in the Pamphylian dialect. In addition to linguistic evidence, on the inscriptions of seven statue bases found in the courtyard at the Hellenistic city gate, the legendary names Riksos, Labos, Calchas, Makhaon, Loenteus, Minyas, and Mopsos are cited as the founders of the city. Linguistic and mythological studies indicate that these names belong to the legendary Achaean leaders who participated in the Trojan wars. After the war, these heroes who did not return to their homeland, aimed to found new cities on the southern coast of Anatolia. Obviously, the Pergaeans who redecorated the Hellenistic courtyard in 120-121 A.D.,believed that the above-mentioned partially historic, partially mythological heroes were the founders of their city. However worthy of respect this belief may be, it does not really prove the city was originaly thus founded. At most, it may mean that the Achaeans mixed with the local people and reconstructed the city.

The period between the Achaean colonization and the Lydian domination is not well illuminated. According to the historian Herodotos, the Lydian King Croesus (560-547/546 B.C.) conquered Perge. Then Cyrus, the Persian king, overthrew Croesus (547 or 546 B.C.) and thus Perge came under Persian rule which lasted until Alexander the Great conquered the city in 333 B.C. Unlike Sillyon and Aspendos that took a hostile stand against Alexander the Great, the Pergaeans seem to have received him warmly. It is even said that Pergaean guides helped Alexander the Great from Phaselis to Perge. The Pergaeans'soft approach to Alexander may not only be attributed to their foreign policy, but also to the fact that the city of Perge was not protected by strong fortifications the way Sillyon and Aspendos were. Perge was fortified against

Sacrifice frieze with the goddess Tyche (Fortuna) from the stage of the Perge theatre. Antalya Museum

Drawn by A. Naci EREN

attacks only during the reign of Antiochos III. (223-187 B.C.) The round tower of the Monumental Gate and the city walls that stand erect today, belong to this time. Following the death of Alexander the Great, Perge was under the rule of Ptolemies of Egypt or the Seleucid kingdom of Syria. With the treaty of Apameia (188 B.C.) the city was left to the Kingdom of Pergamon. Later it came under Roman rule.

The gold plates that decorated the statue of Artemis in the temple of Artemis were plundered by the Roman governor or quaestor Gaius Verres. So says the famous orator Cicero in the prosecution of Gaius Verres in the Roman senate in 79 B.C. A Pergaean doctor by the name of Artemidoros seems to have provoked the looting of the temple of Artemis.

In the second half of the first cent. A.D. Perge was the stage for an important event. In 47 A.D. the first great Christian missionary and theologian, St Paul, came from Cyprus and arrived in Perge via the river Cestros. From Perge, St.Paul went to Pisidia Antiocheia (Yalvaç) and on his return, preached in Perge again. He then headed for Attaleia (Antalya).

Just as it has been for the other cities of the region, the second and third centuries A.D. were a period of prosperity and wealth for Perge. The monumental constructions such as the theater, the stadium, the bath, and the agora that we observe with great admiration today, are products of Perge's second glorious period. The city was represented by the Metropolitan Callinicus at the Council of Nicaea (İznik) in 325.

The Byzantine period, including the 5 th and 6th centuries A.D. constitutes the third glorious period of Perge. The city's religious status and importance caused rivalry with neighboring Side on the issue of becoming a metropolis. As a result, the Church divided Pamphylia into two, as Prima and Secunda, recognizing Side as Prima and Perge as Secunda. This point is also verified by the Council of Ephesos that met in 431 and where Side were represented individu-

1-2 Theatre block with an
   Artemis Pergaia cult image-
   Antalya Museum

4

3   WANESSA PREIIAS
   (one of the local goddess of
   Perge 5th cent. B.C.)
   Antalya Museum

4   Statue base of Kalkhas

- Zodiac Disc with Pergæan Artemis
- Found in Perge, in 1977
- Fine-grained white Marble
- Roman period, 2nd century A.D. Antalya Museum

   Disc surrounded by twelve sing of Zodiac, one sign broken. In the center, bust of Artemis with lunate projections on both shoulders, framed by relief figures of Atlas, river gods and a draped female to the left. Head of bust missing.

ally. After the sixth century, Perge lost its title of metropolis to Attaleia. Between the years 786 and 869 Perge was united with a neighboring city, Sillyon, to form a bishopric metropolis. According to the "Thema" organization that divided the Byzantine Empire on military and civil bases as of the 7 th century, Perge was included in the thema of Cubyraioton. In the 10th century, Perge was still a part of this thema.

From the 7 th century on, mountain tribes, on the one hand, and Arab attacks on the other, caused the weakening of Perge. The development of Attaleia, a neighboring rival city, and is becoming the capital of the thema, too, affected Perge negavitely. Although Perge was still an important city during the reign of Emperor Constantinos Porphyrogennetos (10 th century) starting with the end of the 11 th century, the city became less important and started to decline.

Between the 11 th and 15 th centuries, before the region came under Ottoman rule, Perge changed hands between the Seljuk Turks and the Hamidoğulları. The excavations and research in the area, however, have not revealed any clues pointing to Seljuk or Ottoman settlement in Perge. There is no clear documentation of the date the city was deserted. Most probably the Seljuk attacks from the 12 th century onward destroyed the city which was finally deserted. Historians also deem it possible for life in Perge to have ended as a result of the plague. Or, maybe, until the 18 th century, the city was used as the winter residence of nomadic Turks who moved up to the mountains in the summer and came back in the winter. From its appearance today, it is concluded that Perge was finally destroyed by an earthquake whose date is not known but estimated to have been sometime in the 18 th century.

From the 19th century on, Perge has been a site for research and excavation for many travelers and researchers; consequently there has been a lot published on Perge and the region. Yet the most serious work conducted at Perge is the excavations started in 1946 by Prof. Dr. Arif Müfit Mansel and continued in our day by Prof. Dr. Jale İnan on behalf of General Directorate of Antiquities and Museums, Istanbul University and the Turkish Historical Society (T.T.K.) As a result of the excavations, the city of Perge has regained its present well-organised appearance and thanks to the statues recovered there, the Antalya Museum has come to be an important statue museum. Since 1988, the Perge excavations are being directed by Prof. Dr. Haluk Abbasoğlu. As studied by Prof. Abbasoğlu, the Ionic columns on the Tacituc avenue opening to North side of the Agora have now been re-erected and this pretty avenue has regained its original look. Religious, erotic and social based graffiti figures on the columns make up one of the most attractive sites of the city.

Apart from these, the excavations of the dwelling units by the East walls have renewed the information on civil architecture and showed especially 3-4 cent. A.D. Atrium type dwelling unit a usual architectural style for the region.

Although the actual population of Perge is not known, from the city coins that attribute the city the title of "prote" or "first", it is concluded that Perge was the most heavily populated city of the region.

Pergaean coins, statues, and inscriptions indicate that there were numerous gods and goddesses that were worshipped by the people of Perge. Among these, however, Artemis occupied a special place and enjoyed special importance. Artemis, the main goddess of Perge, was originally known as WANESSA PREIIA in the local language and her origins went back to very ancient times, to the Mother Goddess cult of Anatolia. The cult of the goddess referred to as Artemis

PLANCIA MAGNA

Plancia Magna devoted her entire life and wealth to the welfare of Perge. For this reason, the citizens deified her. They placed her equal to "Artemis Pergaia" and gave her divine honors. Inscriptions found in Perge excavations reveal that Plancia was the daughter of Marcus Plancius Varus, who was proconsul of Bithinia. He erected the triumphal arch in Nicaea (modern İznik, Turkey) during the time of Vespasian. The actual time period, during which Plancia promoted the welfare of the city and presented her many works of art, was during the reign of Hadrian. She was responsible for the oval, court yard behind the Hellenistic City Gate where she placed all the statues of the major gods and protectors of the city into niches of its walls. Behind the court yard she erected a two story triple arch of triumph in the same style as the Gate of Hadrian in Antalya and Athens. She decorated it with statues of emperors from the time of Nerva to the time of Hadrian. She included statues of her husband and nearest relatives. Two statues of Plancia were found; one at the gate of the south Bath another at the Theatre. With the help of these and the third statue shown here we can get a good picture of her portrait and life.

STATUE OF PLANCIA MAGNA

Found in 1969 in Perge between the Propylon of the South Bath and the Hellenistic Round Tower. Fine-grained white marble. Roman, Second century A.D.

Pergaia in the city, was not only worshipped in Perge, but also in neigboring cities, even across the seas (Egypt-Naukratis). The goddess in whose name many reliefs and statues were made, was depicted on city coins, standing in her temple. Under the leadership of the priestesses of Artemis, annual festivities were held. Many ancient writers mention a temple which was "a marvel of size, beauty, and workmanship" and erected in the name of the goddess outside the city, on a high hill. Yet, to this day, the site of this temple has not been located.

The temples of Artemis were holy places of refuge that extended protection to those who sought shelter. It was because of the temple of Artemis that Perge became one of the sacred cities of the region and this occasion later came to be celebrated in the Asyleia Augusteia festival of the city. The annual Syliaia (ΣΥΛΑΙΑ) Games held in the honor of the main Goddess Artemis Pergaia, and the PYTHIAN (ΠΥΘΙΑ) Games held in the name of Apollo were festivals that constituted an important part of the city.

Among the famous Pergaeans, we know of Appollonius-the mathematician and astronomer, as well as Varus, the philosopher. Apollonius (the 3rd century B.C.) believed that objects in space moved in one another's orbits-which we can explain today as the moon's revolving around the earth and earth's revolving around the sun. If the truth behind Apollonius'theorem is considered, one realizes how far ahead he was of his time, for the same theorem and the same ideas were re-discovered and announced centuries later during the Renaissance. The other famous Pergaean is the philosopher Varus (the 2 nd cent. A.D.) who, according to inscriptions, had a statue in the temple of Artemis.

No doubt the most colorful and well-known Pergaean is Plancia Magna, a noble lady who spent all her life and wealth in developing Perge. As such, she was canonized by the Pergaeans and raised to the level of Artemis Pergaia, the patron of the city, to be revered and loved. Plancia Magna who lived during the reign of the Emperor Hadrian, converted the oval courtyard and she placed the statues of the foremost gods and goddess as well as the founders of the city in the niches of the courtyard walls. According to an inscription on her statue, in return for her services, the citizens of Perge named Plancia Magna "Demiurgos" or the highest civil servant of the city, priestess of Artemis, and the Mother Goddess and the Head Priestess of the Emperor's cult.

Dedication inscription of
Plancia Magna

Head of Hermes

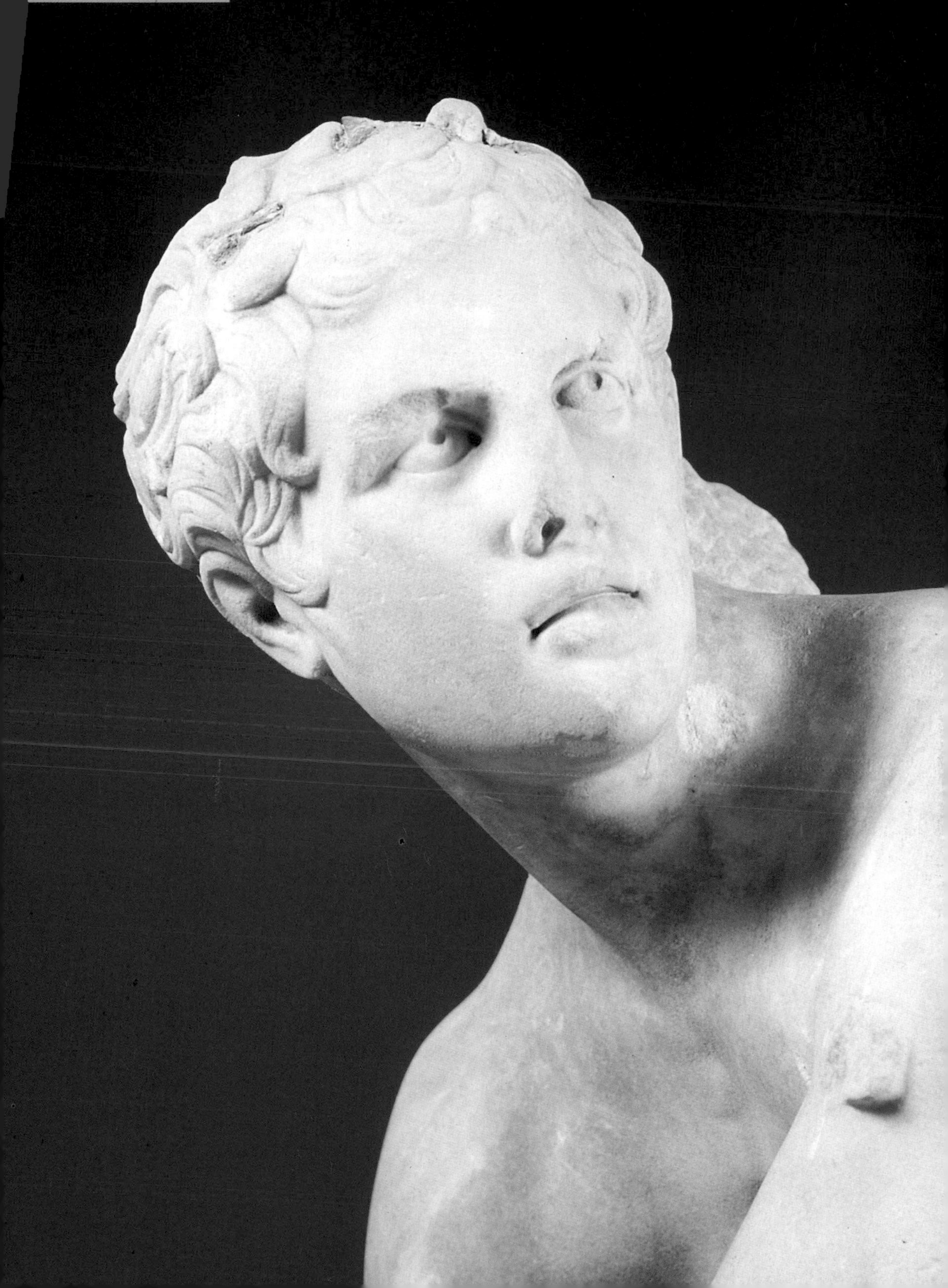

- Statue of a Priest of the Emperor cult
- Found in Perge 1972, in the West portico of the Agora
- Fine-grained white marble.
- Roman, second cent. A.D. (Early Antonine period)

This admirable statue represents a bearded priest of the emperor cult. It has all the characteristics of other statues of priests found in Asia Minor and is one of the best of its kind. He in dressed in a chiton and himation like most statues of philosophers. He is standing on his left leg. His right leg is set slightly forward. His left hand wears a ring with an oval shield. His fingers hold onto the himation. He wears sandals with leather straps on his feet. Typical of priests of the emperor cult, he wears a band with emperor busts on his head. The band consists of a strophion with a ring, decorated with a wide band on which seven busts of emperors slightly damaged are attached. Short straight hair rests on his forehead. His face is wide and square with a moustache engraved by a drill. The hairstyle and beard remind one of the time of Hadrian, but the statue belongs more to the era of 140 A.D.

The city of Perge owed her economic welfare to an even-flowing river that not only connected her with the seas, but also provided the irrigation of the wide lands within her borders where there were large olive groves, vineyards, and cotton fields. There were also surrounding gardens where a variety of fruits and other kinds of produce were grown.

Located on one of the most important trade routes of antiquity, Perge maintained an active economy. The fact that the Pergaeans brought the marble needed for the ornamentation of the city buildings, for statues, and sarcophagi from Proconnesos (today known as Marmara Island, near Istanbul) is an indication of the active trading capacity of the city. Perge's important position in the history of civilization and the history of art stems from the fact she had a notable school of sculpture during the Roman period. The most notable characteristic of Pergaean sculpture-making is the linear and angular style. The shapes are expressed in deep lines.

THE RUINS OF PERGE

The city of Perge was first started on a 60 m. elevation, North of the present day ruins. Known as the Perge acropolis, the area is a wide hilltop whose southern slope is easy to climb while the other sides of the hill are rather steep. Aside from a rectangular cistern, there are no other important remains there that have reached our day.

The Perge city walls and towers are the oldest well-preserved remains. The city walls that begin below the slopes of the acropolis surround the city, sometimes taking minor turns and thus forming an irregular rectangle. The southern walls that were originally connected to the Hellenistic towers, were later taken down when Perge was enlarged in the 2 nd cent. A.D. However, sometime in the 4th cent. A.D., the same city walls were re-erected to include the enlarged city. The rectangular towers of the eastern and western city walls are 13 or 14 m. high. The towers originally must have had three floors and wooden gable roofs.

Reconstruction of the east city tower   1890) Rectangular tower on the east city walls

THE THEATRE

Turning North at the Aksu subdistrict and heading for the ruins of Perge, to the left of the present asphalt road, one reaches the first monumental construction, the Perge theatre. The auditorium of the theatre leans against the Kocabelen Hill to the southWest of the city. The excavations at the Perge theatre which has reached our day in fairly good condition, are continuing. As in antiquity, the entrance to the theatre is through the paradeisos-vaulted entrances on both sides of the stage building. Today, entrance is only possible through the southern paradeisos. The arched entrances, (vomitoria) on both sides, opening onto the horizontal corridor (diazoma) between the seats, as well as, the gate in the middle of the uppermost gallery, provided access to the theatre. With its numerous accesses, the Perge theatre has the region's best plan for spectator circulation.

The Perge theatre, built in the Greco-Roman style, has an auditorium or a cavea consisting of two sections. The lower section has a diameter of 113.50 m. and is slightly wider than a half-circle. There are 19 rows of seats in the lower cavea while there are 23 such rows in the upper cavea. To facilitate access, these rows of seats are interrupted by steps of which there are 13 in the lower cavea and 26 in the upper cavea.

In keeping with the characteristics of the Roman period, this auditorium with a seating

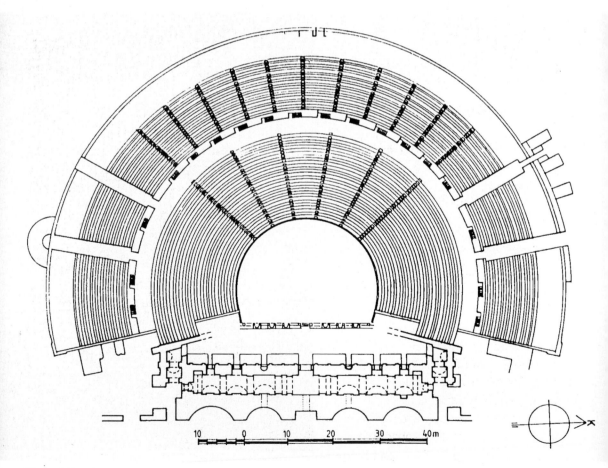

Plan of the theatre

34

capacity of about 14,000 people is surrounded by an arched gallery in the uppermost section of the cavea.

The wide and flat semi-circular area between the stage building and the auditorium is the orchestra section of the theatre. It functioned as a passage that enabled the spectators to reach their seats and the actors to reach the stage building. In the third cent. A.D., the orchestra was surrounded with a marble parapet when the area was used as an arena for gladiator and animal fights.

With its architecture employing columns on levels and friezes decorating the podium in front, the stage building of the Perge theatre is one of the most richly decorated stage buildings in Anatolia.

This decorative richness is also visible on the outer façade of the stage building further indication of Perge's style of luxury. This stage building basically constructed on three levels has five entrances that open onto the orchestra. The large gate in the middle is called "Porta Regia" or the "Royal Door", while somewhat narrower gates are called "Porta Hospitales". Between the gates are podiums on which columns rise. The fronts of these podiums are decorated with high relief friezes depicting the legends of Dionysos, the god of the theatre. On the façade of the stage building there were triangular pediments in between which was a 3 storey columned architecture with statues. No trace of the probably wooden roof has reached our day.

Overlooking the road, the outer façade of the stage building originally had 18 windows. In later periods a monumental semi-circular nymphaeum containing five niches was added to this façade. The columns with red streaks rise above the postaments between the niches.

The architectural pieces recovered, too, point to a rich façade decoration. One meter-high stone railings in front of the first and the fourth niches point to the pools in front of the fountain. Water for these pools was brought through baked clay pipes from the hill behind the theatre.

No doubt, the façade of the stage building of the Perge theatre is one of the finest examples of the Roman period theatre façades that are more ornate compared to the older plain façades. The most eye-catching ornaments of the construction that also serve to create the necessary acoustics, are the friezes that depict the god of the theatre Dionysos' life on the scene from podium.

The visible freezes extend in rectangular panels from the South and from the North towards the center. Each panel depicts a different scene of the life and adventures of the god. However, since the depicted scenes continue towards the center, the compositions on the South and North panels are similar.

Dionysos, the god of wine and the theatre, was the son of Zeus and Semele, the daughter of Cadmos who was king of Thebes. Hera, Zeus' wife, took revenge by asking Semele why she didn't want to see Zeus within all his godly magnificence. He appeared in fire and lightning, burning and killing Semele. Zeus took Dionysos from his mother's womb and placed him in his own thigh. When the days were completed, he took the child out. Out of regard for Hera, he sent the child Dionysos with Hermes to the nyphs to be looked after. Dionysos grew up in the valley of Nysa; as a nature god, he travelled far and wide to teach human beings vine culture and winemaking.

Panel I - On this first panel, there is the young river god Cestros and young women with diadems (crowns) representing the city of Perge. Cestros is depicted half leaning on a rock. His left arm rests on an amphora from which water is pouring out. In his right hand he holds a branch. Opposite this god crowned with a wealth of real grass, stands a dressed young woman, representing the city.

Panel II - This panel tells the story of Dionysos being born from the thigh of his father, Zeus. Zeus seated on a chair extends his right arm to a nymph while his left arm holds the new-born baby Dionysos. The other three figures are of the Nysa nymphs who will take Dionysos under their protection.

Panel III - Upon Zeus' orders, baby Dionysos is entrusted to the Nysa nymphs by Hermes. The cloak over the shoulders of the running Hermes is shown flying because of the swiftness of his motion. Across from Hermes, an active nymph figure holds baby Dionysos in her right arm.

Panel IV - On this panel to the left of the door, the baby Dionysos is bathed by three nymphs. The first nymph pours water from a double-handled amphora into a trough placed on an altar. The second nymph holds a embroidered towel in her extended hands. The kneeling half-dressed nymph holds Dionysos. The baby's face, right leg, and right arm are missing from the frieze today. Dionysos is clad from waist down. The panel is framed with fringes of architectural decorations and displays superior craftsmanship.

On the 5 th panel to the right of the first gate, the Curetes are seen making loud music to prevent baby Dionysos' cries from reaching Hera.

On the very badly damaged panels 6, 7, and 8 between two gates, the satyrs and the nymphs are depicted dancing happily, symbolizing their good life in the Nysa valley.

River - God Cestros
Frieze from the Perge theatre

On the 9 th panel to the left of the second gate, the child Dionysos is seen dancing with three nymphs and Hermes is watching them.

The 10 th panel to right of the second gate, is the best preserved piece of the frieze. It depicts the young Dionysos on a two-wheeled carriage pulled by two panthers. The god's shoulder-length curly hair is parted in two. On his head he wears a wreath decorated with ivy leaves and pine cones. His right hand is raised to his head while in his left hand he holds his thyrsos (staff). In front of his probably wooden wheeled carriage pulled by panthers, there is Pan with a horn amidst his untidy hair. Behind are the Maenads playing the tambourines in their hands. Aside from these, other relief pieces that apparently decorated the stage building are kept at the Antalya Museum; work is continuing on their completion. The reliefs of figures identified as the Lapiths, the Gigants, and the Centaurs, indicate that, just as in many antique buildings, the Perge theatre, too, was ornamented with the friezes about the fights between the Gods and Giants, between the Lapiths, and Centaurs. (Gianthomachi-Centauramachi)

Performances were staged on a wooden platform in front of the stage building, but plays were never as popular among the Romans as brutal gladiatorial combats and races.Theatrical performances were free-only public officers paid for them to gain more popularity and higher office. Roman taste ran to heavy farce with much course language and horse play. Masks denoting comic or tragic roles, long worn by Greek actors, were mostly used for satire by the Romans. Theatre tickets, of metal or bone, were marked on one side to show the seating section and row. These tickets were mostly square or round, sometimes shaped like a fish or a bird.

The definite construction date of the theatre is not known, because the inscription bearing the construction date is heavily damaged. From various indications it is thought that work first started in 1 st cent. A.D., and that the upper gallerys and the additions such as the parapet were made in the 3 rd cent. A.D. Yet, the theatre is generally considered to have been built in the first two decades of the 2 nd cent. A.D. as another gift of Plancia Magna to the city of Perge.

The first restoration work on the Perge theatre was conducted in 1967-68 and the southern analemma wall of the auditorium was restored in those years. The numbered light-colored blocks seen today at the entrance belong to this restoration period. The excavations and restoration work on the theatre was re-instigated by Prof. Dr. Jale İnan in 1985. Thus, a new period for the Perge theatre has begun. Since 1985, the lower cavea and the orchestra have become more organized.The parapet surrounding the orchestra is more complete. New panels of the Dionysos frieze that decorate the podium of the stage building have been unearthed. Of those panels, the one depicting the god's sea voyages is the most striking panel recovered to this day.

The architectural finds of the last seasons are now exhibited in the field next to theatre. Of these, the coffered blocks with reliefs, show superb workmanship and add a striking look to the area. Further-more, the frieze depicting a sacrifice scene is the most important discovery of the recent seasons. In the middle of this frieze, the goddess Tyche is seen holding an idol-like image of Artemis Pergaia in her right hand, thus making the frieze even more important.

By the end of whole study and work; the theatre in Perge appeared to have a three storey front construction. Each store, supported by columns, had friezes lying between and a group of statues, to fit the height of the store, rested in refuges. This group of 17 gods, heroes and emperors are today at exhibition in the hall of Perge theatre in Antalya Museum, open to visitors. One of them is that of Alexander the Great's, with more than 3 meter tall amazing statue to be the only sample known in the world.

Journey of young Dionysos - Frieze from the Perge theatre

Gianthomachi (1),
Centauromachi (2),
Theatre Masks (3)
and head of Medusa friezes from the stage building of the Perge theatre.

THE STADIUM

The barrel vaults located on the right side of the asphalt road extending between the theatre and the city gate belong to the stadium. Almost all of the seats of this 234 meter-long and 34 meter-wide, U-shaped construction are intact, making the Perge stadium the best preserved stadium of the region. The entrance is at the southern end; the horseshoe-shaped northern end of the stadium has no openings.

The seats are arranged on twelve steps that rest on inclined barrel vaults. There are thirty vaults running the length of the stadium and nine vaults at the northern end, with doors in between, allowing access from one vault to the other. At every third vault, there is an opening to the stadium. It can be assumed that these vaults also served as stores or workshops, and that, especially during ceremonies and festivals held in the name of Artemis, the figurines of the goddess were sold there. Forty-two meters of the northern end of the stadium has been walled off to form an arena where gladiator or animal fights were held. The running tracks of this construction that had a seating capacity of 12.000 presently serve as an open-air museum where some of the architectural blocks of the theatre are displayed.

Cross-section of the stadium and the reconstruction of the barrel-vaults

(Lanckoronski 1890)

THE SEPTIMIUS SEVERUS SQUARE

After the stadium, one follows the asphalt road, passes the book-store and enters the city square through the gate dating from the late Roman period. This square, as mentioned earlier, extends between Perge's monumental Hellenistic tower-gate (A) and the gates from the late antique period. (F) Aside from these gates that border the square from the South and the North, the monumental fountain [the nymphaeum of Septimius Severus (E)], the monumental gate [the propylon (D)] that leads to the South bath, and the three niches with statues inside (C) border the square on the West. A colonnaded gallery which is a continuation of the galleries of the colonnaded avenue, borders the area from the East and have a nice designed Roman mosaics on floor

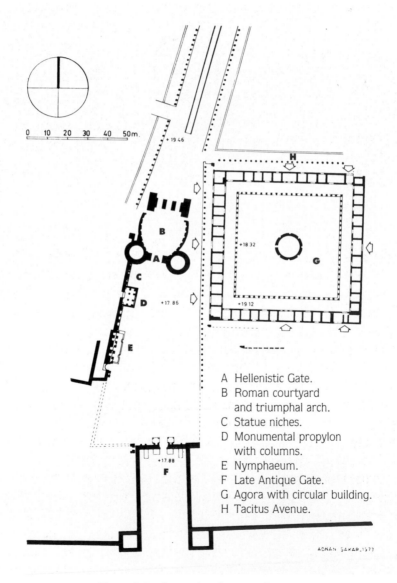

A Hellenistic Gate.
B Roman courtyard
  and triumphal arch.
C Statue niches.
D Monumental propylon
  with columns.
E Nymphaeum.
F Late Antique Gate.
G Agora with circular building.
H Tacitus Avenue.

ADNAN SAKAR 1977

Plan of the Septimius Severus Square

THE AGORA

The square area near the Hellenistic East Tower is the agora of Perge. The sides of this square measure 75 m. In the Hellenistic period, the original Perge agora must have been located near the intersection of the two major avenues at the area known as Cornutus Palaestra today. One of the construction activities of the 2 nd cent. A.D. was the removal of the city walls East of the Hellenistic gate and the building of a new Roman agora there. The agora with one entrance on each side, is basically a square surrounded by Corinthian galleries on two steps and stores behind. On either side of each of the main entrances there are five shops of varying sizes. Some of these shops open onto the agora square, others open to the outside, onto the streets. Because of the natural slope on the South side, the shops had two floors; the first floor opened onto the streets, the second floor opened onto the agora square. The northern portico whose entrance was probably used as a chapel in the Byzantine period, structurally and functionally, displays unity with the Tacitus Avenue in front. Today, only a portion of the mosaics of the gallery and the shops is visible. The game-board at the North gallery is the most interesting discovery made in this area. Right in the center of the agora, there is a round construction (tholos), obviously the podium of a two-level monument whose upper portion has not survived to present. From the finds one may conclude that this construction with a gallery of sixteen columns surrounding it, probably served a religious function much like the temple of Tyche at the Side agora. The Perge agora categorized as a peristyl agora, can be dated to the first half of the 2 nd cent. A.D., similar examples of which are seen in Pompei, Puteoli and Ostia in Italy.

1 Portico from the Agora
2 View of Tacitus street with Ionic columns
3 Graffiti on column

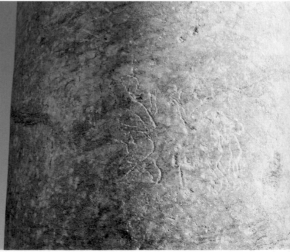

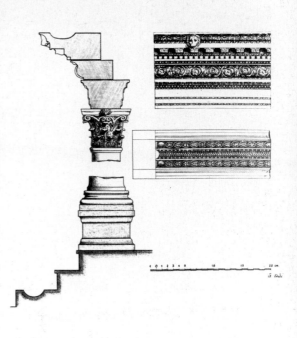

Restored corner from the Agora

A section of an Agora column and architrave blocks

Reconstruction of the circular building (tholos) in the center of the Agora

(A. Dai)

ROMAN ARCH (Late Antique Gate)

Today, beyond the stadium the asphald road leads one to the book store and then to the city gate which is identified as belonging to the late Roman period. In the 2 nd century A.D., in place of this gate, there was a 24 meter-long wall with five large niches on its façade in front of which rested a single-vaulted marble arch as a ceremonial arch for city festivals. The blocks belonging to this arch are still visible on the inner side of the city gate today. When threats of invasion and war re-surfaced in the fourth cent. A.D. the need to build new fortifications resulted in including the façade wall in the city walls and the entrance of the arch was converted into the main gate of the city. From statue fragments and marble slabs recovered, it is clear that the Pergaeans wanted to give this gate a monumental look, too.

Reconstruction of the Roman arch in front of the inner façade of the Late Antique Gate

- Statue of Nemesis
- Found in Perge 1968, in the court of the Late Roman Gate-way
- Fine-grained white marble
- Roman, second cent. A.D.

This statue of Nemesis was discovered at Perge in 1968 during excavation of the court of the Late Roman Gate-Way. It was broken into 14 fragments.

Both of her arms are broken near the elbow. Nemesis is represented in this statue as a tall young woman standing beside a griffon. The weight of the body rests on the left leg and the contour of the hip at this side forms a wide curve. The right leg is relaxed and drawn slightly backwards. She is wearing a peplos made of thin material so that the forms of the body are outlined beneath. The peplos has slipped down from the left shoulder leaving the breast exposed on this side and this producing a folded roll that cuts diagonally across the body. Like a number of other resembling it, the original belongs to the Hellenistic period (2nd cent.B.C.).

HELLENISTIC TOWERS

Approximately 73 meters North of the first gate, between two round monumental towers, stands the second gate of the city the symbol of present-day Perge. Initially, this was the only city gate. The towers constructed in the third century B.C. were four stories high, with windows on the third floor and reliefs of shields between these windows. They probably had conical wooden roofs. Behind this gate lies the oval courtyard circumscribed with walls 11 meters tall. In the early days, there were probably six niches on either side wall, containing twelve statues of the deities. In 121 A.D. Plancia Magna turned this area into a monumental courtyard first adding a niche to the existing row of niches, as well as seven more niches on either side, to form a second level of niches, all adding up to twenty-eight niches. In front of these niches containing statues of the deities, the heroes, the founders of the city, and the members of the Plancius family, there was a two-story construction with Corinthian columns. In the Hellenistic Period the courtyard was truly oval, but in the Roman Period the back wall was taken down to be replaced by a three-vaulted arch reached by four steps. From the inscription of this arch that shows great similarity to the Gate of Hadrian in Antalya, one learns that the construction was a gift of Plancia Magna to the city of Perge. Aside from these two major gates, Perge has two more gates as parts of the East and West city walls.

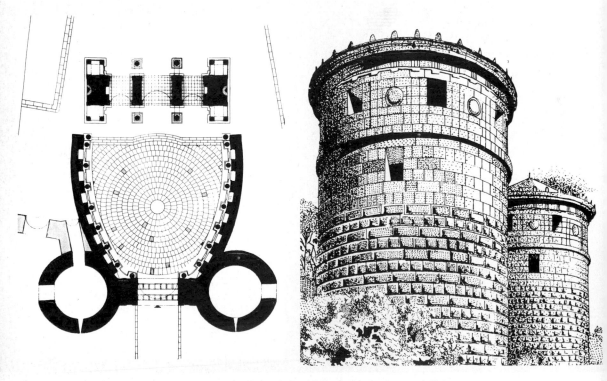

Plan and reconstruction of the Hellenistic towers and Gate-way

THE SEPTIMIUS SEVERUS NYMPHAEUM

The Monumental Nymphaeum, known as the Septimius Severus fountain, is basically a large rectangular pool behind which stands a two-storey façade wall with columns. The upper parts of this brick wall are in ruins, however the lower parts that include five cells have survived to our day. There are two semi-circular basins to facilitate access to the available water. The entire façade, as well as the insides of the cells, was covered with marble. This Monumental Nymphaeum was crowned with a triangular pediment referred to as broken-apex pediment. The reliefs from this pediment belonging to Artemis Pergaia, the There Graces, and Aphrodite are now on display in the open-air gallery of the Antalya Museum. Sculptures of the Emperor Septimius Severus and his wife Julia Domna are among the most important finds of the Nymphaeum.

A short distance from the Monumental Nymphaeum stands the Propylon or the monumental entrance building, giving access to the South bath. Only the foundations and the postaments on which columns stood, survived to our day from this monumental entrance consisting of two rows of four columns and a gate with a decorated frame. These 4,5 m. tall Corinthian columns stood on postaments. They carried a three-level architrave. The most important finds from this building now displayed at the Antalya Museum are the

The reconstruction of the Septimius Severus Nymphaeum   (A. Dai)

reliefs, that decorated the lower parts of the architraves. The Pergacans dedicated the Monumental Nymphaeum to the Emperor Septimius Severus (193-211) and his family.

The last section that borders the square is the three niches between the Propylon and Hellenistic West tower. Excavations revealed that the niches were covered with marble slabs and contained statues inside. The statue of Plancia Magna recoverd from one of the niches is especially important not only because it reveals the portrait characteristics of this noble lady, but also because the inscriptions shed light on the many titles she held in the city of Perge.

The eastern side of the square is bordered by a gallery of columns, 4,30 m. in depth and 96 m. in length. The gallery which portrays different postaments, columns, and column capitals due to frequent repairs appears to be a continuation of the Colonnaded Avenue. In front of this gallery, a wide sewege canal coming from the Colonnaded Avenue, passes by the Hellenistic tower and reaches the courtyard. Access to the South bath, one of the two large baths of Perge, is through the Propylon.

EMPEROR SEPTIMIUS SEVERUS (193-211 A.D.)

Lucius Septimius Severus was born in 146 A.D. at Leptis Magna, Africa as son of Septimus Geta and Fulvia Pia. He was a highly gifted soldier who carried out a number of increasingly important assignments, until he was eventually given the governorship of Upper Pannonia (now N. Yugoslavia). After the death of Emperor Commodus, he declared allegiance to Pertinax, who was later murdered and illegally replaced by Didius Julianus. This caused such a revolt in the various provinces that the troops in Carnuntum declared Severus as emperor. He immediately removed julianus and defeated his third enemy, Clodius Albinus. He told his sons, "Enrich the soldiers, nothing else matters." He was emperor for 18 years by keeping the good will of the army. During his reign, he dedicated himself to expeditions in different areas of the empire and visited several provinces. He founded many colonies, formed three new legions, beautified Rome with new buildings and restored the Pantheon. For the people, he organized a steady and abundant distribution of wheat and other supplies. In 208 A.D. he moved to Britain with his wife, Julia Domna and his two sons in order to conquer Caledonia (Scotland). He repaired the wall of Hadrian after it had been partially destroyed. He died at York on Feb, 4, 211 A.D. at the age of 65. He was cremated and his ashes were transported to Rome, where they were placed in the cemetery of the Antonines.

STATUE OF EMPEROR
SEPTIMIUS SEVERUS IN ARMOR
Found in 1968 at Perge, in front of
the Monumental Nymphaeum
Fine-grained white marble.

EMPRESS JULIA DOMNA
(-217 A.D.)

Julia Domna was born in Emesa, Syria; the daughter of Julius Bassianus and sister of Julia Maesa. She came to Rome as a young woman in 173 A.D. and became the second wife of the Emperor Septimius Severus. She bore him a son in 188 A.D.; the future emperor Caracalla. A year later, she bore another son, Geta, who was also designated as emperor-to-be. She was a woman of outstanding intelligence. Severus frequently consulted her on matters of importance and was guided by her counsel. After the death of Severus, she tried in vain to reconcile her sons, Caracalla and Geta. When she received news in Antioch of the murder of Caracalla, she considered her life to be hopeless and committed suicide by starvation. Her remains were taken to Rome and preserved in the cemetery of Caius and Lucius. Later, her sister Julia Maesa moved her grave and contents into the mausoleum of Antonius Pius.

STATUE OF
EMPRESS JULIA DOMNA
Found in 1968 in Perge, at the
Monumental nymphaeum
between the two main city gates
Fine-grained white marble.
Roman, Third century A.D.

THE SOUTH BATH

The monumental entrance (propylon) in the middle of the buildings to the West of the city square, allows passage to the South-Bath. In the last 15 years, while the South Bath excavations which have formed the focal point of the Perge excavations, have revealed information on the architectural characteristics of the region's bats, the sculptures recovered have provided many clues about the Pergaean school of sculpture. With its side walls intact all the way up to the barrel vaults, the South Bath shows the characteristics of a gymnasium a major attribute of the region's baths. Not favoring symmetry, spaces have been utilized perpendicularly or parallel to one another. As a result of excavations, ten spaces, each serving a different function were identified. Accordingly, space number one at the farthest West point is the bath's caldarium or the hot area. This space overlooks the South through three large arched windows. There is a large pool extending the full length of its southern wall. Below the caldarium there is a 1.75 m. high hypocaust system which served to heat the caldarium. Space number two is the tepidarium, or the bath's warm area, also equipped with a pool and a hypocaust system. Space number three is the bath's frigidarium or the cold area. A large part of this frigidarium is taken up by a big pool that has a canal in front. This canal used to have constant running water for washing the feet before entering the pool. The floor of the pool is covered with white and dark-blue marble slabs. Space number four which contains a large swimming pool was most probably related to the physical education of the youth at the palaestra. In the middle of space number five, there is a pool with a sprinkler system. The largest open-air section of the bath is the palaestra marked as area number six. The palaestra surrounded by a colonnaded gallery on all four sides was an exercise area for physical education. Area number seven is the most interesting area of the bath. The results of the excavations indicate that at least thirty two pieces of sculpture were once displayed here, suggesting the bath was like a sculpture gallery of an art center. On the plinths of most of the statues recovered, there are inscriptions that state they were dedicated by a Klaudius Peison; hence named the "Klaudius Peison Gallery", by Prof.Dr.Jale İnan. Sculptures of a dancer, of Meleagros, Marsyas, Apollo, Nemesis, and Hygeia, all on display at the Antalya Museum today, are finds from this gallery.

To the west of space number eight, there is a pool with a marble floor. Space number nine also has a hypocaust system and space number ten contains the cylindrical sections where cauldrons were placed above the stokeholes.

Monumental entrance (propylon) of the South - bath

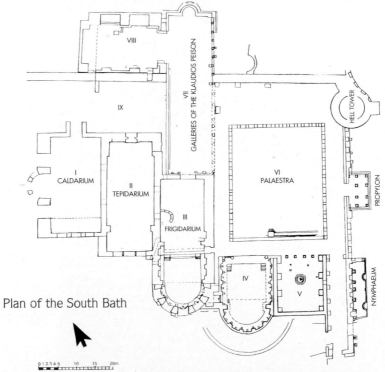

Plan of the South Bath

VIII

IX

GALLERIES OF THE KLAUDIOS PEISON

VII

HELL TOWER

I
CALDARIUM

II
TEPIDARIUM

III
FRIGIDARIUM

IV

V

VI
PALAESTRA

PROPYLON

NYMPHAEUM

0 1 2 3 4 5   10   15   20m

- Statue of Meleagros
- Found in Perge 1981 at the Gallery of Klaudius Peison (İ-7) of the South Bath
- Fine-grained white marble.
- Roman, second cent. A.D.

The statue was discovered in 1981 during excavations in the Gallery of Klaudius Peison (Division İ-7) of the southern Bath of Perge. 47 broken pieces were found and pieces together. The hero is shown as a sad, but handsome athletic young man standing on a large base. The weight of the body is supported on the right leg, the left leg being relaxed, bent at the knee, and drawn back wards.

He is leaning against a lance with the head of a boar at his right side and a dog at his left. He is almost naked. A chlamys cloth is tied with a brooch at his right shoulder.

It goes around his neck and left arm and hangs down to the head of the boar. The original statue of Meleagros by the famous sculptor Skopas dates back to the fourth century B.C. This Roman copy dates to the second century A.D. and is dedicated by Klaudius Peison as indicated by the inscription on the base.

- Statue of Marsyas
- Found in Perge 1981 at the Gallery of Klaudius Peison (İ-7) of the South Bath
- Fine-grained white marble. H.2.00 m. (6 ft. 7 in.) Inv. No:5.29.81

The statue of Marsyas was discovered in 1981 in the Gallery of Klaudius Peison in the South Bath of Perge. It was broken into 16 fragments and restored. The statue is one of a group of three that were found in the area that relate to the musical contest between Apollo and Marsyas. He is represented as a naked-tall man. The weight of the body rests on the right leg and that the left leg was relaxed and extended forward. The lion pelt that covers the athletic shoulders of Marsyas is draped over the left arm with two claws hanging down and the tail reaching the base of the statue. At his right side is a tree trunk on which hangs the flute of Marsyas with its ten pipes. The inscription at the base announces that the statue was donated by Klaudius Peison. The origin of this Perge group is generally agreed to have been executed at the beginning of the 3rd cent. B.C. during the first Hellenistic Period.

THE COLONNADED AVENUE

The Colonnaded Avenue which is the lifeline of Perge, starts immediately behind the Hellenistic gate and ends at the Monumental Nymphaeum at the foot of the acropolis. It is approximately 300 m. long. In the middle, there is a two-meter-wide segmented water canal. On either side of the avenue there are porticoes with mosaics and rows of shops. The water canal in center must have been a source of life for the avenue and the shops, especially on hot summer days. The door lintels of most of these shops are intact; in fact, in the mosaics in front of some of these shops the owners'names are written. A lot of the mosaics, however, are covered with sand in order to protect them. Four columns, about 150 m. from the entrance, rise as the most important columns of the avenue. Most probably these four columns were brought for the narthex of a Byzantine basilica from some other part of the city. The columns are decorated with the reliefs of Artemis Pergaia, Apollo, Calchas, and Tyche. The fact that these columns were erected in a church narthex could well mean that the Christians of Perge identified Artemis with the Virgin Mary and Apollo with Jesus.

The excavations of the Colonnaded Avenue held between 1955-1958 and 1967-1968 have unearthed many inscriptions and sculptures that have provided many important clues shedding light to the history of Perge. A game-board recovered during the 1967 excavations is now exhibited at the Antalya Museum. Consisting of three rows of twelve squares, this board stands as one of the first examples of present-day back gammon.

Columns on the avenue with Artemis - Kalkhas and Tyche (Fortuna) reliefs

Four columns probably belonging to the narthex of the Byzantine church built in place of the shops in the East portico, about 150 m. from the entrance, rise as the most important columns of the avenue. Most probably, these four columns with reliefs were brought over from some other part of the city and erected in the narthex of the church. On the first of these columns the Artemis of Perge is depicted with her scarf and light-emitting crown, necklaces, a torch in her right hand, and a bow and arrow in her left hand. The damaged second relief belongs to Apollo with his crown emitting light and with his carriage drawn by four horses. On the third column, there is a person wearing a toga, holding a flat bowl offering a libation near an altar. The person depicted here could well be "Calchas", the mythical founder of the city. On the fourth relief the goddess of fate, Tyche is depicted with a crown symbolizing the city's fortifications and the horn of plenty in her left hand.

THE DEMETRIOS - APOLLONIOS ARCH

The four-level statue base located approximately the 50 m. North of the four columns with reliefs, and above the West portico must have been an important monument closing off the traffic from the West. At the intersection of the two main avenues of the city there was the Demetrios-Apollonios vaulted arch erected in the honor of Artemis Pergaia and Apollo. Restoration work is being continued on this single vaulted arch that has only two standing pylons and an elevated section for the inscriptions.

Reconstruction of the Demetrios - Apollonios Arch.

Ü. Izmirligil

THE PALAESTRA

Turning West at the juncture of the two main avenues of Perge, one observes the palaestra, a square construction to the North. After the Hellenistic city walls and towers, the palaestra is the next oldest construction in Perge. The construction is made of well-cut rectangular travertine blocks around a wide, open area. Especially the rusticated West wall portrays skilled workmanship. It comprises of a large open space surrounded by various rooms. On the southern wall, there are windows that open onto the avenue. On the North side, there is a construction from the Byzantine Period. According to inscriptions, the palaestra was dedicated to the Emperor Claudius (41-54 A.D.) by a noble Pergaean by the name of C. Julius Cornutus.

THE NORTH MONUMENTAL NYMPHAEUM

Another monumental fountain of Perge is located at the north end of the Colonnaded Avenue and just at the bottom of the acropolis. The U-shaped construction is 21 m. wide and the sides measure 8.75 m. On the long wall at the lower end of the U-shape, there are three niches with that have deep doors and protruding wings. The main fountain is in the center. Below the fountain there is a façade wall with the statue of the river god, Cestros, in front of which lies a pool. Water collected in a tank behind the statue of Cestros flowed into the pool via an opening. The excess water from this pool flowed into the canal running in the middle of the Colonnaded Avenue. The 1970-1972 excavations at the nymphaeum revealed architectural and sculptural pieces which point to a two-floor construction with a very rich façade architecture that was decorated with sculptures.

The inscriptions and sculptural finds unearthed indicate that this construction was built in mid 2 nd cent. A.D. and underwent repair and thus became richer at the beginning of the 3 rd cent. A.D. The statues from the northern monumental nymphaeum are among the most beautiful statues of the Antalya Museum - the statues of Zeus, Apollo, Artemis, and the two Hadrian sculptures, one naked, the other clad, are the most noteworthy.

North Monumental Nymphaeum

(A. Dai)

- Statue of Zeus (Jupiter)
- Found in Perge 1970, at the Northern Nymphaeum
- Fine-grained white marble
- Roman, second cent. A.D.

The statue of the greatest of all Olympians was found from the nymphaeum in Perge, at the North end of the main street. Zeus was decorating one of the niches of the monumental fountain. Six large and six small pieces were broken off that fit together perfectly. Missing are the scepter held in his left hand a finger from his right hand and the globe. His weight carried on his right leg, the left leg being set somewhat back-wards and to one side. He is dressed in a himation over his left shoulder, which extends over his right hip and drops down to his ankle and wears sandals on his feet.

Thick wavy hair and beard frame the face of this god portrayed as a strong adult man. His head is turned slightly to the right. His hair is held with a band around his head. His symbol, the eagle is in front of a support beam next to his right leg. This statue is typical of the classical period (5th cent B.C.) but was made by sculptors Pergeian in the second century A.D.

- Statue of Apollo
- Found in Perge 1971, at the Northern Nymphaeum
- Fine-grained white marble
- Roman, second cent. A.D.

The statue of Apollo was discovered in 1971 during excavation of the Monumental Nymphaeum at the Northern end of the main street of Perge. Apparently it decorated a niche of the Nymphaeum, where 13 fragments were found at the Western wing of the building. The fragments were fitted together at each break. In the reconstruction of the statue missing pieces were filled with Gypsum. He is pictured in this Roman copy of the second century A.D. as a tall naked young man. The weight of the body is supported on the right leg and on this side the contour of the hip forms a strongly protruding curve. The left leg is bent at the knee and extended to the side. His posture facial expression and hairdo remind one of the statues of the Hellenistic period.

Eastern basilica of Perge - 6 th Cent. A.D.

THE RELIGIOUS BUILDINGS

No less renowned in Anatolia then the temple of Artemis in Ephesus, the Perge temple of Artemis is a mythical construction that has kept its mystery until the present. According to ancient writers, the temple "was near the city and located on a fairly high hill,"and it "was a marvel in size, beauty, and workmanship." The temple was frequently depicted on the city's coins. Furthermore, the fact that the famous orator Cicero complained that the gold belonging to the temple was stolen by the region's governor or queastor Verres in 79 B.C., points to the wealth of the temple. Aside from the above-mentioned clues, in 1919, the Italian archaeologist B.Pace's coming across the temple's inventory inscription tablet at the outskirts of the İyilikbelen Hill, south-west of the city, led the research and excavations to this area. Although one Doric and one Ionic temple have been located as a result of excavations conducted in search of the temple of Artemis, the latter still remains a mystery.

Among the city's religious buildings, there were two large basilicas built in the Byzantine period whose remains have reached our day. The first of these is about 50 m. to the West of the monument with steps midway on the colonnaded avenue. Constructed out of re-used material, this basilica with a high apse and rooms on either side of apse, has a well-defined nave and a narthex. The construction technique points to the 5 th cent. A.D. The second basilica is located just East of the late Roman period gate. Only the apse of this 6 th cent. A.D. basilica has reached our day.

THE NECROPOLIS

The first excavations at Perge were started the West necropolis by Prof. Dr. Arif Müfit Mansel. Like all other antic cities, Perge had been surrounded by a large necropolis outside the city walls. After the city of Perge expanded in the 2 nd cent. A.D. monumental tombs, sarcophagi and simple grave chambers, that is, every type of tomb was used. Sarcophagi, however are the most common found among them.

The city of Perge had three major city gates. Many of the tombs were situated next to the roads leading from them. The west gate, also called the necropolis gate, gave access to the city from the west where around found 31 sarcophagi along the road and 3 on the east, 2 on the hillside. Those fine-grained white marble sarcophagi were spaced at a distance of 25 - 30 cm. The inscribed narrow sides face towards the road, some with bases and some without. Some also have integral bases. They are carved with garlands, Medusa heads, Erotes, Nikai and theatrical masks, and some also bear inscriptions. From these inscriptions one can deduce that some families such as Marcii, Aurelii lived in Perge, as well as the last testament of the dead.

They are even inscribed with money penalties which had to be paid to the city treasury if the testament of the dead person was violated. This is an indication of the juridical powers that could be invoked against robbing or reusing a sarcophagus. In such a case the city government was supposed to protect the sarcophagus and impose a fine to be paid to the city treasury if the circumstances required it. Many however, were reused. Changes in the script remind one that re-use of the tombs continued in the Byzantine era. Here is a typical epitaph:

Hello traveller, Ulpius Dionysi(o)s while still alive had a sarcophagus made for myself and my wife, Aurelia Zoe, and nobody has permission to put another corpse in the (sarcophagus) after my death. My heir must seal it with clamps within three days and without any delay. If not, he must pay a fine of 2500 denarii to the city of Perge.

The sarcophagi which stretch from the east gate lie in a field. They are arranged in a row as in the west necropolis. Some of their covers can be seen just above the ground.

The sanrchophagus of Domitias Fliskas - Antalya Museum.

WATER WAYS OF PERGE

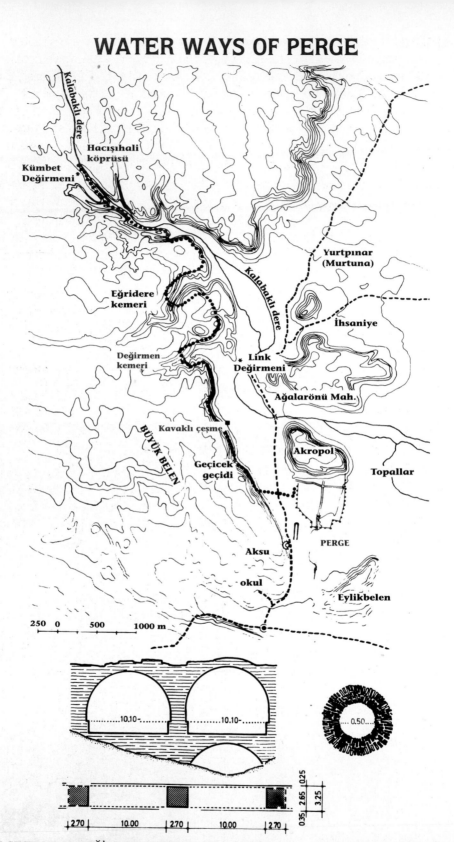

Kalabaklı dere

Hacışıhali köprüsü

Kümbet Değirmeni

Kalabaklı dere

Yurtpınar (Murtuna)

Eğridere kemeri

İhsaniye

Değirmen kemeri

Link Değirmeni

Ağalarönü Mah.

BÜYÜK BELEN

Kavaklı çeşme

Akropol

Topallar

Geçicek geçidi

PERGE

Aksu

okul

Eylikbelen

250   0   500   1000 m

‒10.10‒   ‒10.10‒

0.50

0.025
2.65   3.25
0.35

2.70   10.00   2.70   10.00   2.70

CROSS SECTION OF DEĞİRMEN KEMER (Wheel Arch)

Channel of the "Kavaklı Çeşme"

Ü. İzmirligil

THE AQUEDUCT

With water canals running in the middle of its colonnaded streets, its monumental fountains and baths. Perge is a city with many constructions related to water. These constructions are interconnected with subterranean or surface canals that are partially visible today. The large amount of water necessary for the city was supplied from the North, from the Kümbet Değirmeni on the Kalabaklı Stream.

Passing through open and covered canals and arches, water was brought all the way to the western city walls and distributed to the city by the water gauge near the North bath.

From the Kümbet Değirmeni, the source of Perge's water, the aqueduct first crosses the Eğridere Arch and later the Değirmen Arch before it arrives in the city. The Eğridere Arch is a singular arch constructed of one row of stones while the Değirmen Arch stands on two arches on two levels. The constructions is made of well-cut rectangular travertine blocks. Water carried to the Kocabelen Hill via underground or surface canals was finally distributed to the city by the water gauge outside the western city walls. The Monumental Nymphaeum on the southern slope of the acropolis played the most important role in this distribution.

The Aqueduct of Perge "Değirmen Kemeri" (wheel arch)

ASPENDOS

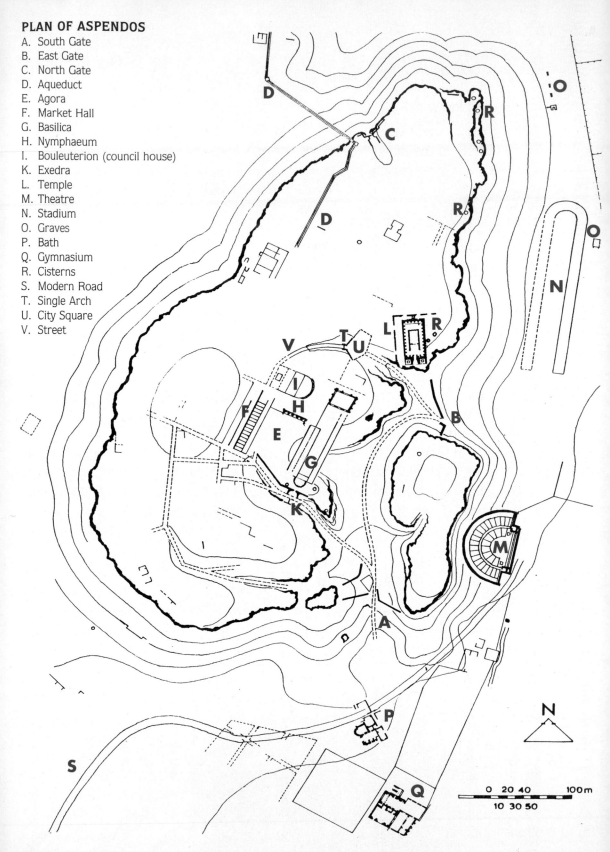

PLAN OF ASPENDOS

A. South Gate
B. East Gate
C. North Gate
D. Aqueduct
E. Agora
F. Market Hall
G. Basilica
H. Nymphaeum
I. Bouleuterion (council house)
K. Exedra
L. Temple
M. Theatre
N. Stadium
O. Graves
P. Bath
Q. Gymnasium
R. Cisterns
S. Modern Road
T. Single Arch
U. City Square
V. Street

N

0 20 40   100m
10 30 50

ASPENDOS

Ancient Aspendos which boast's the best preserved Roman theater in Turkey is well worth a visit for the theater itself and other ruins of the ancient city. It is an easy drive from Antalya and makes a lovely half day excursion.

In antiquity, Antalya and vicinity were known as Pamphylia or the land of all tribes. Aspendos was located on the major crossroads of antiquity. Many ancient writers refer to the importance of the location of the city. The city owed its geographical importance to the river Eurymedon, the largest river irrigating the Pamphylia plains. The Eurymedon emerges from the Taurus Mountains in the North, flows very near the city of Aspendos, and reaches the Mediterranean. Although not suitable for transport today, the Eurymedon in antiquity not only contributed to the fertility of the plains, but also provided Aspendos access to the Mediterranean and offered shelter to ships. As such, the Eurymedon played a vital role in the economic and social life of Aspendos and served in the recording of unforgettable pages in the history of the city.

Just as in the case of Perge, the founders of Aspendos chose a location of fertile plains with a nearby elevation facilitating defence, and a riverside that provided access to the Mediterranean via a river.

Geologically, the Pamphylia region appears in horizontal and perpendicular layers basically formed in the Triassic Period. It is also partially covered by quaternary conglomerates and sand. Going inland, Pamphylia ascends in terraces or small hills. The ancient city of Aspendos was built on such a hilltop. The elevation one sees crossing the bridge over the Köprüçay River or the Eurymedon on the 44 th Kilometer of the present day Antalya-Alanya highway is the upper town, or the acropolis of Aspendos. It rises 60 meters above the plain and covers an area of 20 hectars. It is oval in shape and appears as a flat hilltop. The famous Eurymedon flows about a kilometer East of the city. The fertile lands of the Pamphylia plains spread between the city of Aspendos and Eurymedon.

Between the present highway bridge and the ancient city of Aspendos is the old bridge built during the Roman period under which boats sailed and easily reached the city piers. In place of the Roman bridge whose foundations only have remained to this day, the Seljuks built another bridge in the 13 th century. This latter bridge which has recently undergone repair is still in use.

The fate of ancient Aspendos, like the other neighboring city-states, depended very much on the historic fate of Pamphylia. However, from time to time, Aspendos became the center of events that affected the history of the region. Although no evidence of the existance of the Hittites in the city of Aspendos has yet been found, The "Ahhiyawa" or "Arzawa" land mentioned in Hittite texts is considered to be Pamphylia or in the vicinity, thus attesting to the existance of Aspendos at least as early as the existance of the Hittites. On the Aspendos coins minted between the fifth and third centuries B.C. appears ESTFEDIIYS which indicates that this name belonged to the city or lord of Azitawadi in Cilicia, providing the most important proof of the existance of the Hittites.

ASPENDOS

25   0   25   50   75 Meters

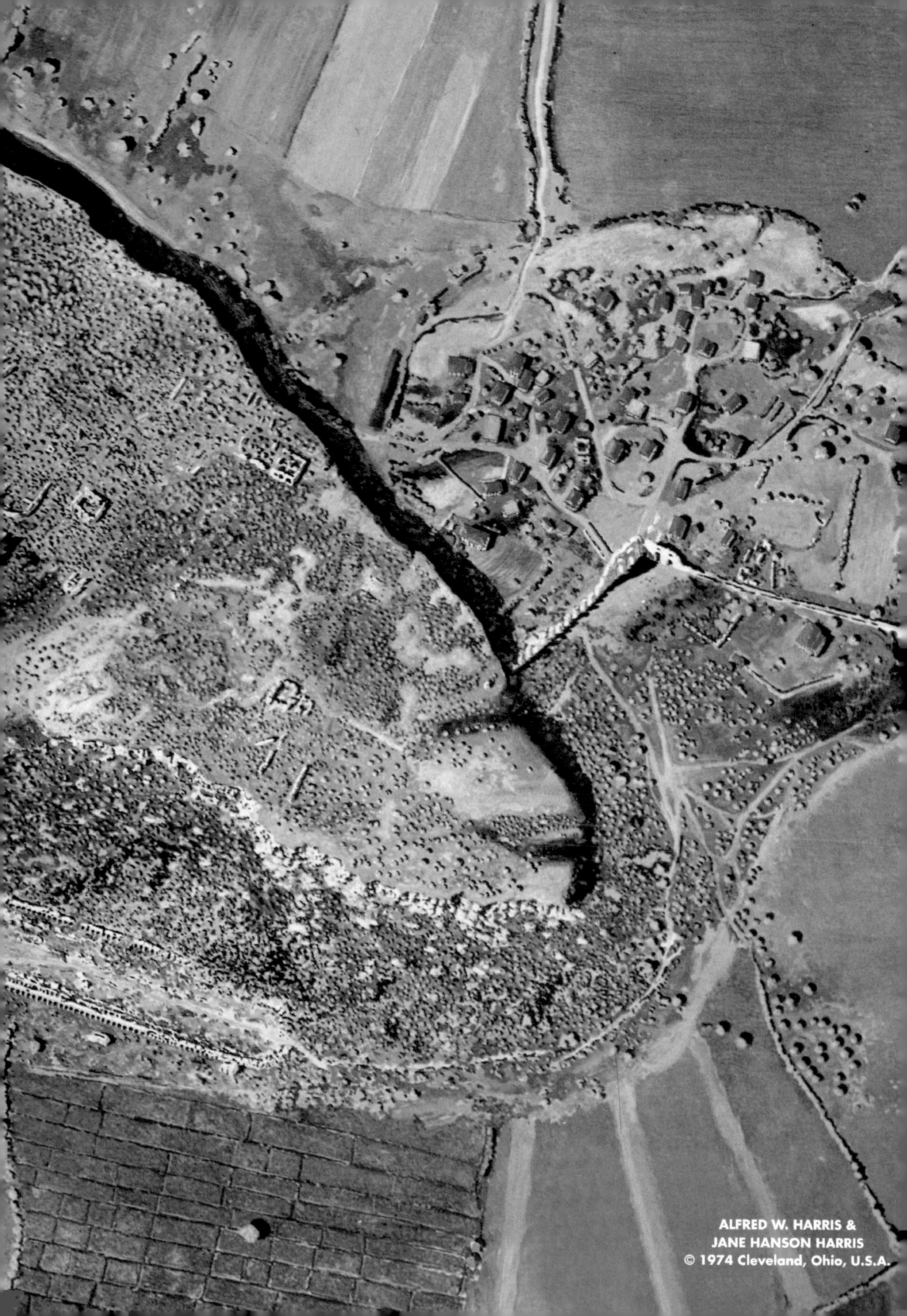

- Red Figured Column Krater
- Found from the Classical
  Necropolis of Aspendos
- Classical Period, end of 5th or begining of 4th century B.C.

Red-figured column-krater decorated with three youths having fun and drinking on one face, and another group of three youths arming on the other. Each picture field bordered above by a kymation. Rays on top of the rim and above the base. Wheel-made.

The Acheans who founded the Mycenaean civilization in Greece in the 14 th and 13 th centuries B.C. expanded to the East Mediterranean to occupy Rhodes, Samos,and Cyprus. During this period the Acheans are known to have also landed on the South-West and South coasts of Asia Minor and that, following the collapse of the Hittite State due to the Aegean migrations from Europe to Asia Minor, they migrated to these shores in large numbers. Greek legends tell about some Achean troops under the leadership of Calchas and Mopsos that reached Pamphylia following the Trojan wars.

The fact that the area was Mopsophia after the leader Mopsos and the fact that ancient writer Dionysos Periegetes (first cent. A.D.) regarded Mopsos as the founder of Aspendos, are considered evidence that strengthen the explanations behind the legendary migration. Similarly, some inscriptions recovered in Aspendos are written in the Pamphylian dialect which seems to be somewhat related to the Achean dialect spoken in Arcadia in Greece. According to legends and from linguistic unity observed, it can be deduced that from 1400 B.C. to 900 A.D. the city of Aspendos was affected by migrations from the West and the local people mixed with the newcomers.

In the eight and seventh centuries B.C. the region faced another migration from Greece. The Greeks were said to have re-established the city as a colony. However, the city name ESTFEDIIYS minted on coins during this period is not a Greek name, but a native Anatolian name, suggesting that the Greeks probaly did not re-establish the city, but rather conquered it and settled there.

Among the colonists' names, reference to "those from Argos" occurs frequently. The ancient writers Strabo and Pomponius Mela also recorded that Aspendos was directly an Argos colony.

The period from the time of this colonization to Lydian domination is a dark one in the history of Aspendos. Aspendos was conquered by the Lydian King Croesos who was later defeated by the Persian King Cyrus, which lead to Persian sovereignty in 546 B.C. However, the fact that Aspendos, together with Side. continued to mint her own coins even under Persian rule indicates that she still enjoyed great freedom. Actually, the Persians did not interfere with the city's affairs; they only taxed the city and appointed leaders loyal to them. In 467 as the Persian King Xerxes, was gathering an army near Aspendos, the Athenian statesman and commander Cimon won victories on this cost. Conquering Carian and Lycian cities under Persian rule, Cimon destroyed Xerxes'navy anchored at the mouth of the river Eurymedon, and succeeded in landing on the shore near Aspendos. Cimon attacked the Persian army a second time on the night of the same day and a statue of victory was erected in his name in Athens because of his double victory in one day. As a result, the Persian threat disappeared and some of the coastal cities joined the Athenian Maritime Leauge or the Delian Confederacy. Though Aspendos was mentioned in a list of the members of the league in 425 B.C., the Persians soon regained sovereignity in the area. In 441 B.C. Aspendos served as a naval base for the Persian governor Tissaphernes who held talks with the Athenian statesmen and commander Alcibiades. In 441 B.C. Aspendos, again appeared as a naval base. In 388 B.C. the Athenian commander Thrasybulos who aimed to regain the prestige Athens had lost in the Peloponesian War, headed for the shores of Asia Minor and

Limestone Honorary Inscription from Aspendos. This inscription is very important because it shows not only that there was a temple of Artemis at Aspendos, but also that even when the city belonged to the kingdom of the Ptolemies it was able to make independent decisions such as this democratic and generous one bestowing citizenship on the foreigners residing there. 3rd century B.C. Antalya Museum.

anchored near Aspendos. Instead of fighting, the people of Aspendos collected money to give the threatening Greek commander. However, the people to Aspendos killed the Greek commander Thrasybulos in his tent because his soldiers had damaged their crops. Thus the people of Aspendos did away with the threat.

.   For nearly a century Persian rule alternated with independence until 386 B.C. when the Athenian Maritime League was overcome by the Spartans, leaving all the cities of Asia Minor to the Persians. The fact that Aspendos and Side, regained their right to mint coins under Persian rule indicates that the Persian domination was actually moderate. Nevertheless, in 365 B.C., together all other Pamphylian cities, Aspendos, too, took part in the unsucessful revolt of the governors (satraps) against the Persian king. Persian sovereignty continued until Alexander the Great's expedition to Asia Minor in 334 B.C. Following the cities of Western Anatolia and Lycia, the Pergaeans, too, received Alexander warmly. According to the historian Arian (the second cent. A.D.) as he later headed East, Alexander the Great was met by messengers from Aspendos who informed him that Aspendos was not going to offer resistence to his forces. The Pergaeans asked him not to leave any garrison in the city. In return for the famous horses of Aspendos, previously also supplied to the Persians, and 50 talents (1 talent was equal to 26.196 kilograms or 57.6 pounds) of gold to be paid annu-ally Alexander went on to Side and Sillyon without leaving forces in Aspendos. During his second attack on Sillyon, Alexander received intelligence that the people of Aspendos were not abiding by the agreement and that they had not only carried all their possessions to their acropolis but also restored their city walls. Leaving Sillyon uncaptured, Alexander attacked Aspendos and captured the lower city and beseiged the acropolis. Realizing they were los-ing the entire city, the citizens of Aspendos made peace agreeing this time to give Alexander 100 talents of gold and 4000 horses annually. In 333 B.C. Pamphylia was united with Lycia within Alexander's empire and its administration was given to an admiral by the name of Nearchos. Following Alexander's death the region came under the sovereignty of Antigonos Monophthalmos. With the defeat and death of Antigonos at the Battle of Ipsos in 301 B.C. Pleistharcos (brother of Cassender, the King of Macedonia) ruled the area for a short peri-od after which Pamphylia was either under the rule of Ptolomy of Egypt or the Seleukids in Syria. In the Battle of Magnesia ad Sipylum in 190 B.C. where the Syrian King Antiochos III fought against the Romans, the Pamphylians sided with Antiochos who later lost the bat-tle. According to the Treaty of Apameia (188 B.C.) that followed the battle, the region was left to a Roman ally, the Kingdom of Pergamon which was later bequeathed to Rome in 133 B.C. leaving Pamphylia free for a period. In 102 B.C. Pamphylia was united to the newly founded province Cilicia.

From the first century B.C. the cities of Pamphylia were constantly under the threat of pirates. In 78 B.C.. the Emperor Sulla appointed Publius Servilius Vita as governor of Cilicia. Servilius resumed the region from a pirate by the name of Zenicetes and joined the area to the province of Cilicia. It is during this period that Aspendos was plundered by the questor, or governor, Gaius Verres who took all statues that decorated the temples and squares. The most renouned statue of Aspendos, known as " the lyre player" also disappeared. We learn these from the famous orator Cicero who prosecuted Gaius Verres before the Roman law courts in 79 B.C.   .

- Statue of Hera Ephesia (Juno)
- Found in Aspendos, in museum since 1926
- Fine-grained white marble.
- Roman, second cent. A.D.

The statue of Hera was one the first to be brought from Aspendos to the Museum of Antalya. With the exception of her missing head, the right arm, and the left hand, her statue is complete and in good condition. The full weight of her body rests on her left leg while the right leg is set gracefully to the side. The goddess wears a long himation coat over a thin and transparent chiton (a woman's armless garment). Her left arm is apparently bent at the elbow and points toward the front,while the right arm hangs straight down. The standing figure as well as the flowing garment show the curves of her body clearly. These characteristics all conform to the style of an "Ephesia" type statue that traces back to the Ionia of the fifth centuryB.C. On the hem of her himation coat are engraved the names of two-sculptors: Moschos and Kallippos from Synnada (Afyon-Şuhut). The statue is also very similar to the replica in Vienna that gave this statue its name. So "Hera Ephesia" is the only statue in the museum that has the artist's name engraved on the garment.

A year after the assasination of Julius Ceasar, Pamphylia became a part of the province of Asia in 48 B.C., but this did not last. In 36 B.C., it was given by Antony to the Kingdom of Galatia. Following the death of the Galatian King Amyntas in 25 B.C., the Emperor Augustus united Pamphylia with Lycaonia and formed a seperate province of the empire. In 43 A.D., the Emperor Claudius this time united Pamphylia with Lycia to form the province of Lycia-Pamphylia. During the reign of Marcus Aurelius (161-180 A.D.) Pamphylia became a senatorial province. The region's affiliation to various provinces during the course of time has been purely on an administrative basis, leaving Aspendos and other cities free in internal affairs but dependent on Rome in foreign affairs.

From the beginning of the Roman Imperial Age onward, Aspendos enjoyed major developments and in this period of peace, the city truly prospered and grew in size. This period of welfare ended with the weakening of the empire towards the end of the third cent. A.D.

In the and sixth centuries A.D. Pamphylia was an province of the Byzantine Empire where Christianity was the state religion. Although Aspendos was not one of the seats of a metropolitan as Side and Perge were, she was still the third largest city of the region. During the Byzantine Period, the name of the city was changed as Primoupolis and Aspendos was under the jurisdiction of the metropolitan of Side. When the Byzantine Empire was reorganized into "thema" or regions, Aspendos was included in the "thema" of Kubyraioton. From the seventh century on, the city was subject to Arab attacks and, from time to time, suffered serious damage.

In the eleventh century the Turks started to conqueror Asia Minor. In the thirteenth century Aspendos was populated by a strong group of Seljuk Turks. During the reign of Sultan Alaeddin Keykubad the stage-building of the Aspendos theater was remodelled and

Silver Stater of ASPENDOS
400 B.C.
OBVERSE : Two naked wrestlers
REVERSE : Slinger in action to left ΕΣΤΓΕΔΠΥΣ to right, triskeles

Seljuk tile from the stage building of the theatre at Aspendos. 13th cuntury - Antalya Museum.

Composed of star-shaped underglaze-painted tiles decorated with floral motifs blackish blue on blue ground and small square tiles with bird, inscription and floral designs in cream on blue ground at four corners of each star-shaped tile.

used as a palace. In the fourteenth century the city of Aspendos was under the rule of Anatolian princes, but from the 15 th century onwards she was under reign of the Ottomans. Aspendos was most probably abandoned after a severe earthquake in the eighteenth century. Although there has been no excavation at Aspendos, since 1924, the city has become one of the most important archeological sites of the Turkish Republic. In the nineteenth and twentieth centuries the site has been the focal point of many scholars whose publications have helped to make Aspendos world-famous.

No doubt, Aspendos owed her fame and welfare to the River Eurymedon, the present-day Köprüçay. Thanks to the Eurymedon, the city has frequently been the most important military base and the most important commercial center of Pamphylia. Aside from her fertile plains, the nearby olive groves, vineyards, and saltbeds, as well as, the grain farming and horse-breeding in Aspendos played a big part in city's trade. That Aspendos minted the most convertible coins of the Mediterranean from the fifth century onwards has been interpreted as a sign of her important role in trade.

Among the most important exports of the city were rugs, kilims, weavings, and textiles, as well as, furniture made of the wood of the lemon tree. According to the ancient writer Strabo, the salt derived from the now-dry Lake Capria and the high quality Aspendos wine were popular on the mediterranean markets. The fame of the horses of Aspendos throghout the ancient world is proven by the tax of 4000 horses per year which Alexander

Seljuk bridge over the Eurymedon. Re-erected in the 13th century.

levied. As a city state, or "polis", Aspendos was ruled by three assemblies, the "Boule", the "Demos" and the "Gerousia" representing the officials, the citizens, and the elderly respectively. From a third century B.C. inscription containing a ruling of the demos, it is understood that this assembly had the authority to issue citizenship to foreigners. In the Roman Period, on the other hand, the same assembly is shown on city coins as having the right to construct temples on behalf of the emperor.

The city's golden era coincides with the Roman Period, that is the second and third centuries A.D. The spectacular theater and the aquaduct are priceless monuments from that period.

Although the population of the city is not known for certain, it is clear that Aspendos was one of the most densely populated cities of the region, ranking as the third biggest city after Side and Perge.

Among the famous citizens of Aspendos recorded in history, one can cite the name of Andromachos who lived in the third century B.C. and who served as commander in the army of Ptolemy IV. The Pythogorean philosopher Diodoros is another well-known name from the city.

According to a third century B.C. inscription, Artemis occupied a very special place, apart from the other gods and goddesses in Aspendos and there was a temple of Artemis.

THE GYMNASIUM AND THE SMALL BATH

The two ruined buildings on the right side of the road before reaching the theater are the bath and the gymnasium. Of these constructions the smaller one closer to the square to the North has characteristics of a Roman bath. The arches and vaults of this construction are made of the well-cut conglemerate blocks and mortared rubble and bricks. The building was composed of four large areas: the changing room, or the apodyterion, the cold room or the frigidarium, the warm room or the tepidarium, the hot room, or the caldarium, which were all covered by vaulted arches. Since no excavation has been conducted in this building it is difficult to name each of the spaces. A large portion of the partition walls seperating the chambers as well as the terra-cotta pipes running through the vaults and the walls, have survived to our day. The technique of construction points to the third certury A.D

The other construction with vaulted arches near the bath is the city's gymnasium. In harmony with the architecture of the region, this construction consists of chambers parallel or at rigth angles to each other in an asymmetrical plan. The overall plan is practically square. Comprised of a courtyard in front, a hall at the back and other spaces, the construction is made of well-cut conglomerate blocks with mortared rubble in between. Bricks are used for the vaults and arches. The façade of the building faces the North-East. The wide open courtyard here is the exercise hall, or the palaestra, behind which is the long, rectangular hall that must have contained sculptures in the niches in its walls. Behind this front area, there are the classrooms, the changing rooms, or the apoditerion, and the various sections of the bath-namely the cold area, or the frigidarium, the warm area, or the tepidarium, and the hot area, or the caldarium. Because the area has not been excavated yet, it is not possible to identify each space definitely. Today, only some parts of the partition walls and some of the terra-cotta pipes for hot and cold water and steam-heating, have survived. The construction technique of the gymnasium point to the third cent. A.D.

THE THEATRE

Following the bath and the gymnasium one reaches the theatre-the symbol of present-day Aspendos. Among the monuments of the Pamphylia region, it is the only construction over which everyone from ancient writers to present-day tourists and writers, agree as the most perfect as well as the best preserved example of the last stage of Roman theatre architecture. The building is constructed on the Eastern slope of the small hill on the East, one of the two hills the city was built on. Today, the asphalt road reaches the entrance of the theatre, making it the most accessible ruin of Aspendos. Present-day visitors enter the theatre in much the same way as spectators of the ancient times, through the parados that connects the stage building and the auditorium. The paradox are side entrances with vaulted arches. Two other small doors on the slope that are closed off today were also used to permit spectator circulation in the theatre.

With all of its architectural features, the theatre of Aspendos displays all the true characteristics of a Roman theatre. Even if the theatre were built in earlier times, the present construction which covers all such remains, does not leave behind any earlier clues.

Just like any ancient theatre, the Aspendos theatre, too, has three main sections:

1. The Auditorium: The auditorium is the section where the audience sat. It has a semi-

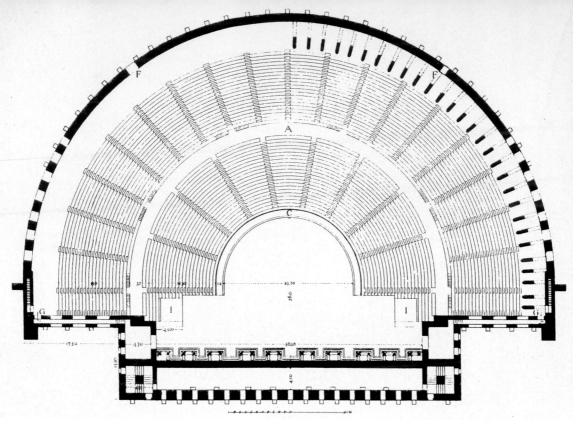

Plan of the theatre

circular plan with some seats arranged on steps that recline on the slope of a hill.

However, a large portion of the auditorium, especially the upper rows, rest on vaulted arches. The auditorium has an upper and a lower cavea, each separated from the other by a horizontal passage called the "diazoma." There are 20 rows of seats in the lower cavea and 21 rows of seats in the upper cavea, each made of marble-like, quality limestone blocks. The steps that divide the two cavea perpendicularly are positioned somewhat lower than the seats in order to make it easier for the spectators to go up and down. There are 10 such steps in the lower cavea and 21 steps in the upper cavea. The topmost row of seats is bordered by a gallery composed of 59 arches. This gallery which seems to have been added to the theatre some time after it was originally completed also served to provide shelter from the rain. The bricks and fragments of columns used in the construction of the arches reflect the restorations made in the Seljuk Period, whereas the white blocks in the lower cavea depict restoration work conducted in recent years. The vaulted gallery on the diazoma level extends right around the lower cavea. Such a gallery was a mandatory architectural device that provided support for the upper cavea. Names inscribed on some seats indicate that there were reserved seats for some special people. Private boxes for the elite of that city, the family of the emperor, and the priest of Vesta had seats over the two side entrances, the paradox. Entrance to these boxes was either through the stage-building or through the doors that connected the lower cavea to the outdoors. The first row in the auditorium was reserved for senators, judges, and ambassadors while the second row was for the elite and

the high military offices of the city. Women sat in the top seats below the vaulted gallery. The other sections of the auditorium were open to all citizens. It is difficult to give definite numbers as to the seating capacities of ancient theatres since they each varied in size, but the Aspendos theatre must surely have had a seating capacity of 15 or 20.000.

2. The Orchestra: Between the stage building and the auditorium, the semi-circular orchestra is the center of the theatre. Present-day visitors arrive in the orchestra right after entering the building. Originally, the orchestra provided actors access to the stage building and the audience access to the auditorium. The original stone blocks of the orchestra, which had a radius of 24 meters, as well as the water canal around it, are still in good condition in some places. Water that might accumulate in the orchestra section is channelled out from under the stage building via two channels. In the third cent. A.D. the orchestra was circumscribed by a stone parapet in order to be able to have gladiator or wild animal fights.

3. The Stage Building: The stage building is standing today. The very top blocks of stone are equal in height to the upper arches of the auditorium. The two-storey construction is made of well-cut conglomerate which is local to the area. The five entrances to the

Reconstruction of the stage building (Lanckoronski 1890)

lower floor which connect the orchestra and the outside were used by the actors. The large central entrance is known as "porta regia" or the "royal entrance" while the two smaller entrances on either side are referred to as "portae hospitales" or gates for the guests. The much smaller doors below these were used to let the wild animals out into the orchestra during gladiatorial combats. The same doors also served to control the acoustics of the theatre. The present tower-shaped entrance is a Seljuk addition. There are four rows of windows of varying sizes and shapes above the entrances. The high arched windows of the second floor of the building. There are projecting blocks above and below these top windows. The upper blocks are pierced with holes while the lower blocks have sockets. Similar projecting blocks also appear on the outer façade of the auditorium. These served to hold the poles of the temporary awning.

The interior of the rectangular stage buildings is like a high and narrow corridor connecting the theatre boxes in the two adjacent constructions. The stage building was composed of several sections; however, partitions have not reached our day. The Aspendos theatre displays the most harmonious unification of a stage building and an auditorium.

The inner façade of the stage building was entirely covered with marble and displayed extremely rich decoration. It had forty-standing columns on two levels almost all of which have disappeared; there are only some fragments left behind in the walls. The lower columns were Ionic while the upper ones were Corinthian. Behind these columns, on the actual wall

there were numerous niches with pediments supported by smaller columns. In these niches stood the statues that decorated the building. Unfortunately none of these statues has reached our day. In a large pediment above the upper row of columns stands a figure of Dionysos, the God of theatre and wine, surrounded by women twigs and flowers.

The outstanding feature of the stage-building are traces of the Seljuk Period. If the theatre has been well-preserved to this day, it is thanks to the Seljuks who used it as a palace. The precious examples of Seljuk tiles from that era displayed at the Antalya Museum today.

In antiquity plays were performed on a wooden platform in front of the stage-building. These were either the performances of order Greek tragedies and comedies or Roman dramas and comedies. The most popular of all were the Roman comedies employing heavy farce with much coarse language. Actors used leather masks depicting the parts they played. They usually wore long-sleeved outfits and long boots or their daily attire.

Upper gallery of the theatre

"Carmina Burana" Summer night performance at Aspendos

However, during the Roman Period the most popular activities held at the theatre, were the gladiatorial combats and wild animal fights. The orchestra of the theatre was circumscribed to be used as an area for these fights.

Citizens were free to give performances in the theatre. The necessary expenditure was partially offset by official organizations which naturally later claimed a portion of the profit as revenue. Spectators purchased tickets to watch plays or races. The tickets were made of metal, ivory or bone. They carried different symbols as well as the numbers indicating the rows and seat numbers. These tickets which were mostly round or square were sometimes shaped like a fish, a bird, or even a piece of fruit.

The Aspendos Theatre was most probably built during the reign of Marcus Aurelius (161-180 A.D) by the architect Zeno, son of Theodoros. An inscribed statue base located in the South parados and two meters above the ground level explains that the citizens of Aspendos have erected a statue and made a gift of a piece of land near the stadium as an expression of gratitude to the architect Zeno for his valuable contribution to the city. The theatre which was presented to the city by two brothers, Curtius Crispinus and Curtius Auspicatus was dedicated to the Imperial family and the city gods. Today the Latin and Greek inscriptions above the side entrance are only partially visible.

Stage building and detailed corner of the Aspendos Theatre

THE STADIUM

On the east slope of the acropolis, the area to the North of the Aspendos theatre, belongs to the Aspendos stadium. The U-shaped construction that extends from North to South occupies 6450 square meters 215 m x 30 m). As in the Perge stadium, the seats of the Aspendos stadium were supported by barred vaults and the entrance is on the short side on the South. Only a very small portion of the arches and the spectator seats have survived to our day.

THE AQUEDUCT

After the theatre, the second most spectacular construction in Aspendos is the aqueduct which was built to bring water to the city from the North. A good portion of this aqueduct is well-preserved and as such is the finest example of Roman aqueducts that exist today. The system includes an arched bridge between two towers, one located on the slopes of a hill on the North, the other near the acropolis. On both towers there are pools to collect water. Under normal atmospheric pressure the water collected in the North tower was channelled via the arched bridge to the South tower from where the water was distributed using the same principal to the city. The aqueduct is made of well-cut square conglómera blocks that are lined with a pipe system carved out of limestone blocks.

Both pressure towers are approximately 30 meters high and have staircases providing access to the top. The arched bridge that extends between the two pressure towers is 880 meters long, 15 meters high, and 5.50 meters wide. During the times the plain was a swamp, the bridge also functioned as a medium of transport. An inscription records that a man by the name of Tiberius Claudius Halicus presented the aqueduct to the city of Aspendos. The system of waterways is dated to the second half of the second cent. A.D.

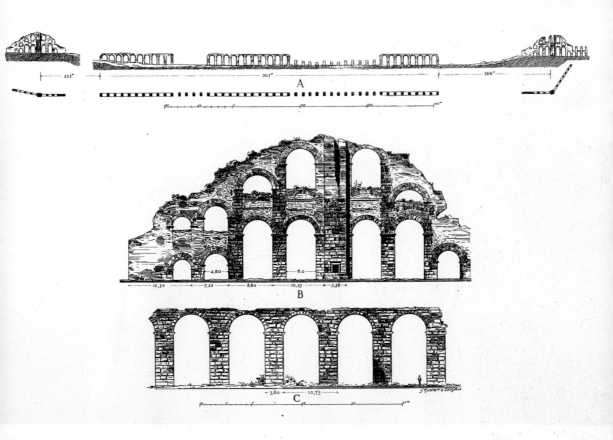

A cross - section of the aqueduct

(Lanckoronski 1890)

A view of North (1) and South (2) towers.
Aqueduct of Aspendos (3).

THE ACROPOLIS

The large hill West of the small elevation on which the theatre leans is the acropolis. A path at the back of the theatre provides easy access to this site where the city was first developed; however today there are no visible remains of the original settlement. What now remains belong mostly to the Roman Period or later periods.

The acropolis is about 60 meters above the plain and covers an area of approximately 20 hectares which is partially circumscribed by city walls and their monumental entrances. As such there is an appearance of an inner fortress with the city walls covering the slopes where defence could be somewhat weak. The strongest fortifications stretch on either side of the city entrances of which three in annuity. These were the East, the North, and the South entrances. The East gate which was on the slope between the theatre and the stadium provided the easiest access to the city center; only a very small portion of this gate now remains. The North gate is located at the point the aqueduct entered the city; it is mostly buried under the earth. As for the South gate, it is to the South-West of the small elevation the theatre rests on. Most of the South gate is also buried under the earth. Some of the outstanding constructions that have reached our day at the Aspendos acropolis are the nymphaeum or the monumental fountain, the bouleuterion or the council hall, and the shops belonging to the second and third centuries A.D. There are also a number of rectangular and pear-shaped Hellenistic and Byzantine cisterns on the acropolis.

THE AGORA

The agora of Aspendos occupies the widest space among all the ruins found on the acropolis. Different from the Side and Perge agoras, the Aspendos agora is not symmetrical in plan and does not have a gallery surrounded by columns, or does it have a temple in its center. Most probably, the Hellenistic agora was used in the Roman Period, too, with several additions that did not change the original plan. The basilica and the exedra on the East, the nymphaeum, or the monumental fountain, and the council hall, or the bouleuterion, on the North, and the marked hall or the shops surround the agora.

At the top of the street that starts at the South gate and leads to the agora, there is the exedra which served as the órators's platform. It is rectangular in plan and on the side that faces the street there is a semi-circular cell whose walls were originally made of marble slabs. The cell is covered with a semi-circular dome. On the inner walls there are five equidistant niches that once held statues.

The ruins at the North-West of the agora belong to the city's council hall or the bouleuterion. The building which was probably also used as an odeion or the music hall, is rectangular in front and semi-circular in the back. Well-cut conglomerate blocks were used in the construction that also includes rubble masonry in between. The beam holes in the walls suggest that there was a roof.

To the West of the agora there is the market building . The shops extend 70 meters on a podium that rises a few steps above the level of the agora. Presently there are only twelve adjacent stores that are separated by well-built walls of conglemerate blocks.

New Discoveries in Aspendos
CITY SQUARE - SINGLE ARCH WAY - STREET and the TEMPLE

Excavations, restorations, and environmental works in Aspendos, the name of which has been encountered in many ancient sources, and which has been the subject of researches of many travellers and scholars since the eighteenth century, have been done by the Museum of Antalya since 1990.

Works have formerly been started by making paths to be able to climb up the acropolis easily from the theatre.

During the researches mentioned above, one part of the main street linking the city to the agora from the Eastern Gate, the single-monumental arch on the street and the small square in front of the single-arch and the ruins of the temple lying on the hill to the West of the stadium are the new discoveries of Aspendos.

The path leading to the West from the Eastern gate probably follows the traces of one of the main streets of the city. The single-arch which the path reaches is the proof of this idea. For this reason, the small square and nearly 75 metre part of the street of the city have been able to be discovered during the excavations done both at the front and at the back of the single-monumental arch. The traces of restorations of different period of time and re-used blocks prove that the acropolis of Aspendos was re-built in a planned way in the third cent. B.C. and the main street and the square were used until the end of Byzantian period. The sewage channel passing through the middle bottom part of the street, which was made from carefully cut rectangular blocks, proves that the city had a planned drainage and sewerage facilities.

Prof. Dr. Jale İNAN in Aspendos Excavations August, 1992

The monumental single-arch having been built with lime stone on the base of local con-glomera blocks and the statue bases in the surroundings show that the square had quite a rich decoration. So this richness is the indication of the Roman period in the mid of the sec-ond cent. A.D.

In the excavations done on the hill to the West of the stadium, one of the temples of Aspendos has been discovered, which is very important as this construction is the oldest mon-umental of the city as well as being the remains of the first temple.

The temple was 24.30 m. long and 13.20 m. wide, but only its triple stepped stylobate platform, the entrance ramp, parts of the wall of the cella, and the square pedestal of the statue have been preserved.

The foundations and walls, were made of local conglomera and lime-stone blocks and roof was covered with brick tiles.

The triglif-metopes, architrave blocks which have regula and guttaia and other architec-tural pieces show that the temple is a small one in the Doric order with 6 columns on the front and 11 columns on the flanks dating at the end of third or beginning of the second cent. B.C. Thus the chance has been captured to be able to have information about the histo-ry and the architecture before the Roman period with the help of the temple which is at least 400 years older than the magnificent theatre of the Roman period.

The temple stands on quite a large temenos area covering a flat topped hill and the wall blocks of temenos with carefully cut conglomera blocks seem to be in a good condition in the Northern side. Three pear-shaped cisterns were found in the interior of this area as well.

The finds; excavated in this area make us think that the Hellenistic temple was sur-rounded with the Roman portico.

1-2 View from the Doric temple

3 Architectural pieces of the Doric temple. (Architecture and triglif - metope blocks).

4 Plan and façade of the Doric temple

3

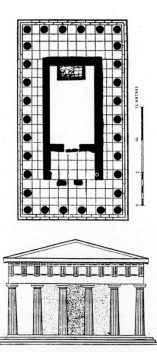

4

Remains of the basilica

THE BASILICA

The basilica located to the East of the agora used to serve as the city trading office and hall of justice. 105 m x 27 m construction consisted of three main sections composed of a central hall and two adjacent halls. What remains of the basilica today are the foundations of the conglomerate blocks used for the partition walls and their supporting vaults. The apse at the South end of the building is a Byzantine addition indicating that the building was used as a church in the Byzantine Period. The sections between the vaulted parts of the foundation were converted into a cistern during the same period.

The monumental square construction at the Northern corner of the basilica is one of the rare buildings that has remained standing to this day. The official or legal affairs were

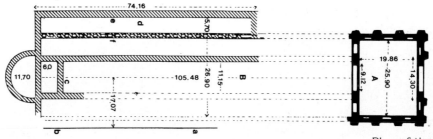

Plan of the basilica

carried out in this section of the basilica which is fifteen meters tall and made of con-glomera blocks. The construction has three entrances, one in the North and two in the South opening onto the basilica. On the inside of the East and West walls there are three niches each of which must have held sculptures.

THE NYMPHAEUM

The most noteworthy construction bordering the agora on the North is the monu-mental fountain or the Nymphaeum. The construction that is 32.50 m. long and 15 m. tall is the most majestic of all the agora constructions that have remained standing. It is made of well-cut rectangular blocks of conglomera the inner surface of which is plain. The outer façade, however, displays a two-storey architectural feature. On each storey there are five niches. The central niche on the first level was later used as an entrance. The building was entirely decorated with marble slabs and statues in the upper inches. In between the lower level niches Corinthian columns on bases supported the architraves and blocks of friezes. As such, the façade of the nymphaeum was architecturally rich in decoration. The water for this monumental fountain was supplied from the aqueduct by two channels in the back.

Remains of the nymphaeum, 2nd century A.D.

SİDE

THE HISTORY OF SİDE

At the end of a 3 kilometer asphalt road, a South turn on the 75 th km. of the main road from Antalya to Alanya, Side appears on the very edge of a small outlet into the sea. As it was one of the major sea ports of the time, it is now a popular tourist center in Turkey. In other words, the city has become the victim of its own popularity.

According to ancient geographer Strabon and historian Arrianos, Side was first settled in 7 th cent. B.C. as a colony to West Anatolian city of Kyme but when Kymeians were not able to colonize local residents they became assimilated and forgot their own language. At that time in Side the language was a distinct form of the Anatolian language, Sidetan, which has still been worked upon. In this language, the word "Side" meant "the pomegranate that symbolizes the fruitfulness"

As the furthest East settlement of Pamphylia, today it is not very obvious whether Side was first settled by colonists from Kyme of Aeolia, as we do not know whether it is true that Aspendos was first settled by the Greeks of Argos. All we know for sure is that the Greek immigration to the region, following 1200 B.C. is after the immigration to the Aegean region. Yet, the Greek immigration must not have been so dense because as ancient writer Arrianos states, for the invasion of Side by Alexander the Great, Kymeians forget their mother tongue on settling to Side and developed a distinct local version. This local traditional story somehow explains that the Greek population had not been large in number and had then been assimilated by local residents. It is fairly clear that Kymeians were neither colonists nor invaders but were immigrants and did settle as Metoikos, namely unregistered citizens. That is why Side had never been colonized by Kymeians contrary to verdicts of ancient writers. This is proven by another theory that there was no link between Side and Kyme as it frequently happened between the main city and colonies. This is the same with Aspendos which was neither a colony nor an establishment to Argos because, except for Attaleia, all Pamphylian cities had been named long before Greeks. The name "Aspendos" well fits ancient Anatolian names as it is suffixed with "nd" that belongs to Asia Minor languages. As for names Perge and Side, they are not Greek. These three cities are now accepted to be ancient Anatolian settlements Aeol or Argos immigrations would not mean colonizations or invasion.

The city, in 6 th cent B.C. was under the domination of the kings of Lydia until they were defeated by the Persians. Nothing is known about Side during the period of Persian rule. In 334 B.C. the city surrendered by Alexander the Great without any resistance. After his death, (until 218 B.C.) Pamphylia was ruled by the Ptolemies of Egypt, then it became the control of the Seleucid Kings of Syria. In 190 B.C, Side was the scene of a battle between the fleet of the Syrian King, Antiochos III, commanded by celebrated Hannibal from Carthaga and that of the Rhodians who were the ally of the Romans, which is known to be the Side naval battle in recorded history. Side supported the Seleucids against the Rhodians in 190 B.C. In the Apamea Treaty, Side veined forces with the Seleucids and were defeated in the Magnesia Battle between the Kingdom of Seleucids and the Romans in 188 B.C. Side was given to the Kingdom of Pergamon who supported the victorious Romans in the battle. It did not last long and the city regained its independence and starts its best period. Side appears to have avoided falling under the rule of Pergamon, and enjoyed a substantial degree of independence in the middle of the 2 nd cent. B.C. It entered a period of growth and prosperity, and become one of the most important trading cities in the East Mediterranean and a centre of culture and education.This was a wealthy period, obvious with the coins of the city that have a pomegranate symbol on one side. Antiochos the 7 th, the heir to the throne of the Syrian Kingdom, came to the city for his education. This is another indication of Side's progress in art and culture in that period. Unfortunately, its citizens did not always have a very good reputation. When asked to name the most unscrupulous people, the wit stratonicus replied "In Pamphylia the men of Phaselis, in the whole world the men of Side." Pirates from Pisidia and Mountainous Cilicia in 1 st cent. B.C., riot some places in Mediterranean region with the help of Pontus king Mitridates the 6 th. According to Strabo, Side became deeply involved with piracy, allowing them to sell their prisoners in the city and to repair their ships in the harbour. This situation changed when Roman Council P.Servilius Vatia clears the pirates from the region in 78 B.C. This also connected Side to Rome and further became to an Imperial city in 25 B.C. After the 2 nd cent A.D. it becomes the capital city to the state and began a second progressive period. Many fine buildings whose ruins may be seen today were constructed in this period.

Side has though days in the end of 3 rd and 4 th cent. A.D. when Northern settlers (Isaurian tribes) crusaded down. However, the Sidetans repaired the city's defenses and during the reign of Julian (361-363) successfully resisted a siege by the Isaurians.

Relief of the pomegranate as a symbol of SİDE.

- Silver Tetradrachm from the hoard of Side
- W: 16 gr.
  247 - 180 B.C.

OBVERSE: Helmetted head of Athena to the right.
REVERSE: A Standing Nike holding a laurel-wreath, to the left; pomegranate and letters ΛR.

By the 4 th cent. A.D. Gods of the city, Apollo and Athena were replaced with Christianity. The city became a religious center and the seat of a metropolitan bishop. Side again became an important commercial centre in 5th and 6th cent. A.D. Finally this is what makes Side enjoy its last strong period.

Arab pirates attacked the city to destruction in 7th cent. and in 9 th and 10th cents. the city was burnt to a cinder.

Constantine Porfirogennetos (913-959), the emperor to Byzantian called Side a Pirates'nest. İdrisi, an Arabian Geographer, mentions Side as Antalya the cinder and adds that people immigrated in a two days walk away from Antalya after the city was burnt. The city after the sovereignties of Seljuk in 13 th cent., Hamitoğulları and Tekelioğulları in 14 th cent. becomes a probe of Ottomans temporarily in 1391 and permanently in 1422. However it was not until islanders immigrated from Crete in 1895 that Side had any Turkish settlers. Side was once a serene village of Selimiye, yet today it is a bustling and sophisticated tourist center without necessarily thinking whether this change has rightly deserve.

THE HARBOUR

Being be the busiest port in the Mediterranean Sea made Side an important city in ancient time. In other words, what kept Side's economy and wealth going was its open markets into Mediterranean's trade. Coins from Side are clear evidence that even Attaleia competed with Side. These coins, were signed by many of the cities governed by Bergama and then reissued into circulation which simply mean the recognition of the value of the money. It was the same in Kyzikos, Rhodes and Lycian cities. Tetradrahmi, then was found everywhere in East Mediterranean, Asia Minor, Syria, Egypt and so on. Side consecrated its trade all in Mediterranean and Aegean seas. That is why Side needed a strong navy force beside the strong trade lines. Five of the warships from this navy force had sided in Roman forces during the third Carthaganian battles (149-146 B.C.) and played important roles in vanishing the Carthaganians fleet.

The port, is thought to have been constructed in Hellenistic period, and was located on the South-East bank of the peninsula. Great portion of the remains which then extended to the port is today covered by new settlings and sand. Some of the Port's walls can today be seen among the orchards.

The mouth to the port was a ten meter wide opening of a pier with walls. The pier, home for fishermen today, is still seen underwater. In its time the pier was filled with debris and garbage after a stormy weather rested and it was so difficult to clean up the pier that this later became an idiom for complex work like "to turn out to be pier in Side". When settlers found the cleaning work painstaking and time consuming they switched the pier to a new one in 5 th cent A.D. in the West bank.

Side extends along a main avenue cutting the city through on a peninsula into the Mediterranean Sea. Today covered by modern roads and dwelling units the avenue was then a huge block of rocks and had been rimmed by a water canal. Another avenue to South after the main gate is now resting beneath the sand expecting to be uncovered although it was severely destroyed during the Byzantian period.

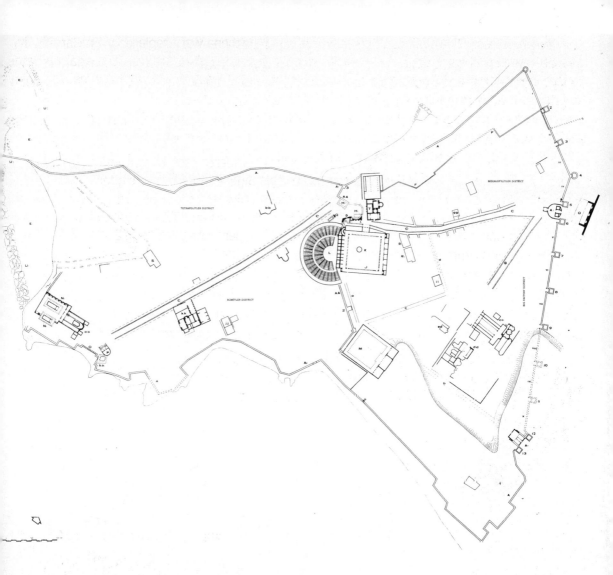

THE CITY PLAN WALL and GATES

In antiquity, Side had four large districts surrounding the main streets of the city. The vicinity of the main gate was called (Megalopylits), the West of the theatre (Tetrapolits), South of the theatre (Bomits), and the East of the theatre "Big Factory". Even Sides' narrowest streets still possessed an excellent sewerage system, and were nourished with lots of water. The main water of the city was supplied from the Dumanlı gorge, the source of the Manavgat River (Melas), which is now submerged under the waters of the Oymapınar Dam.

Water, was brought through an aqueduct and tunnels a distance of 29 km to the city from the Dumanlı gorge, it was stored in the principal cistern which is to the North of the theatre and was conducted to the city via stone and terra-cotta pipes.

Side was surrounded on the landward and seaward sides by walls erected during the

Hellenistic period. The wall on the South which faced the sea has almost entirely disappeared. The walls were repaired during the late Roman period. The land walls stretching to the North-West and South-East have almost been best preserved until now. On the walls constructed of rectangular-shaped pudding-stone without the use of any mortar stand 13 towers of rectangular-shaped towers. On the first two storeys of the three-storeyed walls are the paraphets and look-out posts for soldiers,on the third storey are the embrasures (epalksis) used for shooting arrows. On the walls on the landward side stand two monumental gates. The one known as the great gate was constructed during the Hellenistic period. It has been largely destroyed until now. The gate consists of a courtyard with a plan of semi-circle between two rectangular areas both at the front and at the back. The two rooms which are rectangular in shape stand on both sides of the area at the front.

The gate was protected by two rectangular towers on either side. Inside the inner walls of the middle courtyard, were transformed into a courtyard of honour in the second century A.D., there are chambers and the surface is covered with marble slabs. The surface was decorated in columnar architectural design a two-storeyed gallery can still be seen today. The parts of the capital and other pieces belong to that architecture.

The East Gate , which was discovered in the East part of the city was completely covered with sand, this dates back to the Hellenistic Period. It consists of two passage ways of which the upper parts are covered with barrel-vaults and a rectangular-shaped courtyard with the gates at the rear.

On either side of the courtyard adjoining the walls are the staircases. A frieze of weapons in relief were discovered on the terrace walls of the entrance. These reliefs depicting the loot which the Sidetans acquired after a victory are still displayed in the open-air gallery of Side's museum.

The wall dividing the city in half on the narrowest point of the peninsula belongs to the period in which the city impoverished in the 4 th cent. A.D. The wall stretching away through the skene building of the theatre is also known to be Philippus-Attius Wall.

In Side two honourable epitaphs belonging to Helena, who was the mother of Constantine (324-337) have been found.(Helena passed away in A.D. 327)

There are few epitaphs for Helena in Eastern Greek. Therefore these two epitaphs of sanctification in Side are extremely important. The two epitaphs belonging to the Queen are considered to be a sign of importance of Side. Helena might have visited the sacred city, Side on the way back from a pilgrimage. According to another legend, the boat of the Queen was caught in a terrible storm while coming to Pamphylia from Constantinopolis after the Queen had found the cross of Jesus Christ in Jerusalem. When the boat was about to sink, she had thrown a pin into the sea. Thus, the storm stopped and the boat was drifted into the harbour. After this event, Side (the Gulf of Antalya today) has been called the Gulf of Helena since then.

The other epitaph is known as the sanctification epitaph. In that one, the followings are written.

"Side, the metropolis of wealth sanctifies the Queen Helena, the mother of the King."

Monument of Vespasianus

NYMPHAEUMS and BATHS

The three-storey edifice situated across the main gate, outside the city walls is the Nymphaeum. It was erected in the mid 2 nd cent. A.D. Today, two of the original three-storeys remain standing. It is 50 metres in length and has a rectangular shape. The front part consists of a high wall with three niches and a large basin which is 10 metres in width. The niches were covered by half domes and the water was pouring through the grooves inside the niches into the front basin.

The front wall was covered with marble slabs and decorated with three-storeyed columnar architecture. In the space between the columns and the parapet of the basin there are reliefs depicting various mythological scenes. The one of these reliefs depicting Ixion being punished by stretching on the wheel is now displayed in Side's Museum.

No water supply (Castellum) was found behind the splendid Nymphaeum. The water is assumed to have been carried by terra-cotta pipes from the aqueduct nearby.

The people gathered in front of the nymphaeum on an area once paved with marble slabs during the oppressive heat of summer to relax and to be cooled by listening to the sound of the pouring water. Now, access to the museum is by an asphalt street which once used to be a colonnaded one, following the monumental fountain and the entrance. It is possible to see the gates of the shops which have not yet been excavated on either side of the colonnaded street. The museum of Side was originally an agora baths constructed in the 5 th cent. A.D. The rectangular building in shape, was converted into a museum after being restored, and consists of five sections.

To the West of the Agora Baths is the oblong-planned palaestra, to the West of the palaestra is the agora surrounded by shops, both in the North and in the South. Access to the baths was by the frigidarium (cold section) which was used as the apoditerium (changing room) as well. To the North of the barrel-vaulted building is the basin which was filled with cold water. Some inscriptions at the bottom of the basin belonged to the ancient buildings and they were the re-used materials that built the baths. In the middle of the hall is the base of a basalt column, the oldest structure (7 th cent. B.C.), which has been discovered up to now . The base was used as the altar in the temple of Apollo. The reliefs depicting arms and armour were discovered in the East gate of the city are now displayed along the South wall.

The second section covered by a dome is the sweating room or the lokonium. Small finds are displayed in the windows.The third section is the Caldarium, in other words; the hottest section of the baths. The section surmounted by barrel vaults was constructed of conglomera blocks and was covered with marble slabs. Two large basins facing each other are in their original condition but three small basins were added at a later date. The heating system is seen beneath the floor covered with marble slabs. In this hall, statues, reliefs, objects that related with burial customs which date from the 2 nd or 3 rd cent. A.D. can be seen. From the caldarium one gained access to the tepidarium, through a narrow door which is the warm section of the baths. From this section which was barrel vaulted one could reach the other tepidarium through a door which is now closed, and then onto the frigidarium. In this hall, the statues, which were found during the excavations in Side, are displayed. Among them, the most important finds are the statue of Hermes, the head of Hermes and sarcophagi.

Apart from the Agora Baths, which is now the museum of Side, the other two important baths are in a good state to visit. The one named the "harbour baths" is situated on the North-East corner of the first harbour. It was constructed during the 2 nd cent. A.D. and is the oldest bath of Side. This one consists of 10 sections which give access to each other through small doors. The sections were covered with barrel-vaults and largely remain standing today. The biggest Baths of Side are located in an area between the South side and the colonnaded street. It was constructed in the 3 rd cent. A.D. and restored during the 5 th and 6 th centuries. It consists of 8 sections which largely remain standing.

To the South-East is the agora surrounded by two rows of shops. To the West is the palaestra which was constructed of conglomera blocks. The sections covered with the slabs of marble were barrel-vaulted. On the friezes, which the columns in front of the entrance in the North were surmounted by, the figures of the nereids and tritons having "eros" on their back parts. These friezes are displayed in the North of the courtyard to the museum. Just next to the museum is the fountain consisting of three basins on the colonnaded street. Between the basins, inside of which were covered with marble-slabs, were the statues on the high pedestals. The statue of Hermes, displayed in the museum and the head of Hermes were found here. To the West of the triple-basin fountain is another fountain with a circular basin. The general plan was a big niche with a semi-circular dome. The road passes under a Roman monumental arch which may have been surmounted by the quadriga that gave its name to this area of the city. Just opposite the fountains are the Vespasianus Monument which is next to the monumental arch which is now the Gate. The monument, restored in 1962, was used as the fountain by being carried from its original place while the later period city wall was being constructed. Thus; the Sidetans imitated the city's original big gate and the fountain next to the monumental arch which was transformed into a gate in a way. The monument consists of a large semi-circular niche between the two pediments. On one of the architrave blocks, it is written to have been dedicated to the Emperor Vespasianus and Titus (74 A.D.) There were statues in the niche before it was transformed into the fountain.

THE AGORA

The large area opposite the museum is the main agora of the city. The South side of the area of which access is by the colonnaded street linked the passage ways of the vaults to the theatre. In the middle of the agora are the circular temple which was dedicated to the goddess of fortuna or, Tyche. The temple which was circular in shape was surrounded by 12 columns and covered by a pyramidal roof. The podium and the roof cassettes of the construction, which date back to the 2 nd cent. A.D. remain standing today. On the stone rows of seats of the latrium which placed South-East corner of the agora was covered with vaults. Beneath the rows of seats was the sewerage system and clear water was flowing through the small channel. Lined with marble panels, it had 24 scats positioned over a water-cahnnel.

The walls of the construction were covered with the slabs of marble and vaults with mosaics. The marble slabs in the agora are originally from the stage building of the theatre.

To the South-East of the main agora is the "State Agora". The section which there are columned galleries and shops between both the agora and the wall was almost entirely destroyed during the 4th century while Philippus Attius wall was being constructed.

The state agora was in rectangular shape and surrounded on four sides by colonnaded porticos. In the centre of the agora was the base of a giantic size cross erected during the Byzantine Period. The construction behind the East portico of the state agora is believed to be the hall of the Emperors. Especially, the central part of the construction consisting of three section was elaborately decorated. The two-storey building was surmounted by the statues in the niches. It dates back to the 2 nd century. A.D. and it is thought to have been used as a library.

THE THEATRE

To the South of the main agora is the theatre of Side. It was constructed on the narrowest part of the peninsula and is the only sample both in Anatolia and in the Mediterranean world with respect to its plan and its technological features. Despite the other theatres constructed on natural slopes of the hills, the main construction of this theatre was supported with the vaults arches and columns.

The auditorium where there are seats has a double cavea. The cavea is divided by a diazoma as a horizontal passage. Below and above the diazoma are of 29 rows of seats. Unfortunately, 22 of the upper rows of seats have now remained.

The lower section was divided by 12 radial staircases, the upper cavea by 25 radial stairs. The first storey and the outer galleries of the storey-vaults on which the upper storey rises have now remained standing. This gallery consists of 14 shops and 5 entrances. The entrances consisting inner gallery and lower section provided access to the upper section.

The orchestra planned in semi-circle between the stage-building and the cavea is surrounded by a water channel. Beneath is the sewerage system draining rain-water away. During the later Roman period, it was used as an arena after the wall surrounding the orchestra had been raised. Furthermore it was converted into a basin by plastering the outer space of the wall. Thus; the Sidetans were able to perform the plays related with naval battles. During the Byzantine period, the chapel constructed next to the orchestra and the area was used as an open-air church. Opposite the orchestra is the three-storey splendid stage building. The lower passage ways of the stage building also providing acoustics link the orchestra and the agora. The surface of the platform was decorated by a friezes depicting the life of god Dionysos. During the Byzantine period,reliefs were entirely damaged. On this platform there are decorations of the stage building of the three-storey column architecture design. The stage building, which has suffered considerable damage until now, is in a very good state of repair. It can be said that the foundation was constructed during the Hellenistic period and the theatre which today remains standing was built in the 2 nd cent. A.D. The remains of the foundation on the North side of the theatre belong to the temple dedicated to Dionysos, the god of wine and theatre. The edifice which is Puseudo-Peripteros-planned was buit during the Hellenistic Period and restored during the Roman Period. Thus; it was used besides the theatre.

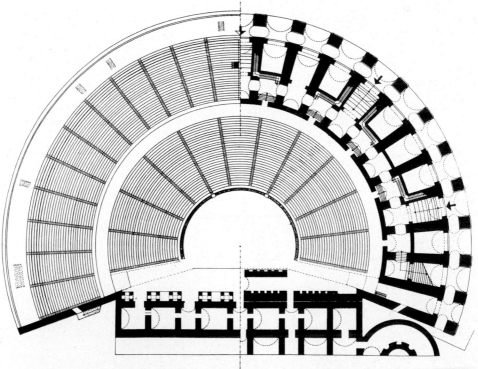

THE TEMPLES

Without doubt, the most interesting remains of Side are the temples erected on the Southern end of the peninsula. The Sidetans had erected two magnificent temples dedicating to the city's main deities Athena and Apollo. Both the temples are in the peripteros plan, in the Corinthian style, had 6 columns on the front and on the back and 11 on the sides. The columns rise on a three-level platform. The entrance to the pronaos was flanked by two columns. There was no opisthodomos. The columns of the West façade of the temple of Apollo supported an architrave and frieze of Medusa heads and actors' masks. The course of restoration of this temple was started by Prof. Dr. Jale İnan and 5 of the columns have been able to be raised until now.

The temples erected in the 2 nd cent. A.D. are in the courtyard of the basilica constructed during the Byzantine period and they were badly damaged. The basilica next to the temples is a three-apse one. At the end of the middle nave there were also syntranon which have six marble steps. On the either side of the apse are the pastolerion rooms (store rooms) in the South, a martyrion was added at a later time. Inside the basilica, which was badly damaged in a fire, was a church constructed at a later date.

On the square at the end of the ancient colonnaded street there was the temple of Men which has semicircular plan. He was an Anatolian moon god often linked with Attis. Access was by a monumental staircase to the temple rising on a high platform.Like the others, this temple too was erected during the second century A.D.

We have been able to have enough information about the ancient houses of Side, discovered during the course of excavations. The first of the houses is in the North of the still stands agora, on the main street. The gate of the house leads to the entrance room called vesti-bulum. To the right of the room of which the floor was covered with geometric designed mosaics is the cellar. The two-storey building was constructed during the Roman Period and was used during the Byzantine time. It is called the house with consoles because of the travertine consoles supporting the upper floor.

Opposite the house with consoles is the house with peristyle due to its plan. It consists of a central courtyard and the rooms surrounding by. The central courtyard is covered in mosaics and has a well. Both of the houses have excellent running water and sewerage systems. This represents the architecture of the type of the house with consoles of the Mediterranean, world still used today.

Side was a city of which the people were amply supplied with water. The water supply of the city was brought a distance of 29 km to the city from the Dumanlı source by means of tunnels, channels and aqueducts. This source is now submerged under the lake of the Oymapınar Dam.

Apart from the two-storey Akçay arch, all the others were one-storey. The arches were constructed of rectangular conglomera blocks. Water brought to the West of the inland walls entered the city by means of the aqueduct built of high arches and then it was stored in the main cistern behind the theatre. The water from the cistern was distributed throughout the city by stone or terracotta pipes as well as being distributed to the baths and fountains. The excess water was used for the sewerage system.

Temple of Apollo

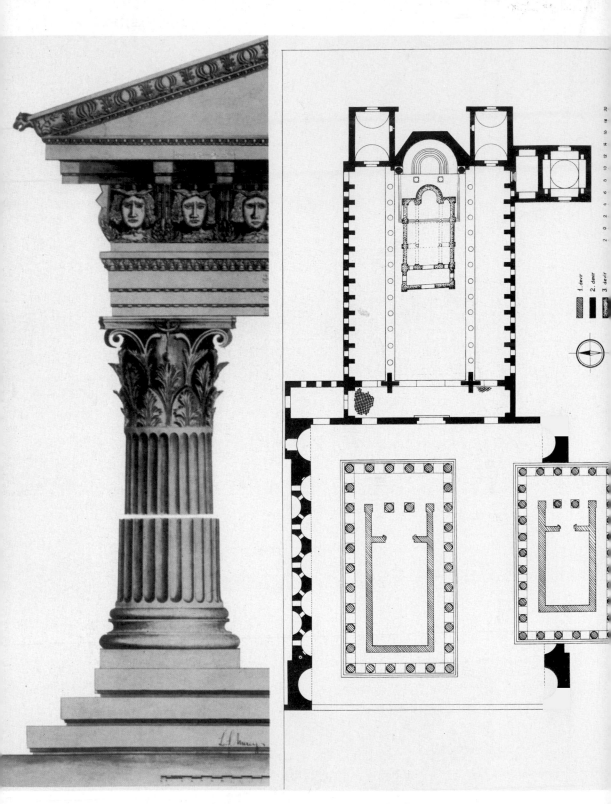

Plan and reconstruction of the temples

Restored corner from the temple of Apollo
Head of Medusa

The reconstruction of the library

THE NECROPOLIS

Outside the city walls lies the necropolis. The necropolis, occupying a large area between the Eastern and Western shores, consists of every type of grave from simple tomb to ostotheks (cinerary urns), many of the fine sarcophagi and monumental mausoleum. But today many of them are covered by cultivated land. Among the sarcophagi discovered there, Garlanded, Sidemara, Attica and Pamphylian style now displayed in the museum. An eagle, some instruments of war such as armour and weapons belonging to one of the monumental mausoleums can be seen. 400 meters from the area on which the seaward lands and the inland walls connected is a magnificent monumental mausoleum known as the "West Mausoleum". The mausoleum standing on a high podium is in the shape of four columned temple in the front. There were sarcophagi inside of the mausoleum covered by marble slabs. To the East, on the main road leading to Sorgun stands there was the second monumental mausoleum. Much of this has almost entirely been destroyed. The sarcophagus with the drank Eros figure which is now displayed in the museum was found in this mausoleum. Finds discovered here reveal that the necropolis was used during the Byzantine Period.

The course of excavations in Side , which many travellers and scholars were attracted by in the 18th and 19th century, was started by late Ord. Prof. Dr. Arif Müfit Mansel 1947 to the name of the Archaeological Department of Istanbul University and Turkish Historical Society. Prof. Dr. Jale İnan took over from Prof. Mansel. As a result of the excavations having lasted until 1967, the remains, which can today be visited, were discovered and many finds exhibited in the museum were discovered. Excavations related with the theatre and the temple in ancient Side have not yet been completed, it still continues so we will confine ourselves to those which have so far come to light.

THE AQUEDUCT

In ancient times, the water supply system of one of Pamphylia's most important ports Side, was a very ingenious engineering structure. The most worthwhile section of this incredible engineering feat has been entirely absorbed by the 4 km lake of the dam. The water supply line in a narrow gorge from which the arched dam has been constructed is a steep rectangular channel hollowed out of the rocks and which crosses the valley of the Manavgat river. The people of Side had constructed a very small dam at the Dumanlı gorge 100 m from the exit of the underground river over the Manavgat river and had carried the water from steep place, sometimes by building an aqueduct on shallow ground, and sometimes by cutting the hard rocks like cheese to create tunnels.

They built very high arched and two-storey aqueducts at one spot between the village of Homa and the district of Manavgat. This 29 km long water network was one of antiquity's most incredible feats, but unfortunately, as mentioned above, the most interesting aspects can no longer be seen.

Considering that in antiquity Side was known to be a very important slave marked, this 29 km long network is thought to have used a lot of slave labour.

The water network fed the nine fountains with three drinking basins each of the semi-circular.

Nymphaeum which can be seen at the entrance to Side, and which is a monumental fountain building. From here the water was carried to the pools in front of the building and from there through channels distributed to all parts of the city. The Nymphaeum was built in the 2 nd cent. A.D., and it is believed that the water way was constructed at that time.

The actual source of the Manavgat stream is 29 km to the North in the Taurus Mountains and it emerges from a gorge where there are very steep sides, almost right angle. This spring is one of the world's greatest carstic formation sources. The magnificent view presented by the world's biggest underground river will no longer be seen by anyone, because it has now been absorbed by the Oymapınar dam's lake 4 km away.

The water from the Dumanlı cave emerges very rapidly, under great pressure and like a syphon a name given to this kind of spring by the French for the famous Vaucluse type spring where the water emerges from the depths under great pressure.

The water in the Dumanlı underground river is fed by the doling, pole and sink holes in the closed river basin of the Taurus Mountains. However as the source of the water is not know the place where it emerges remains under the lake of the dam. This magnificent cave which is now only in photos is submerged beneath a layer of water 120 m in depth. It was the biggest underground river in the world.

One of the tunnels on the Side waterway. (1)
Remains of the aqueducts in the vicinity of the Dam Lake. Kırkgöz (2) and Akköprü (3).

Remain of the aqueduct in the vicinity of the Dam Lake.

Repair
inscription
of the
aqueduct

The aqueducts of Side which were destroyed because of either natural catastrophes or battles have been tried to survive by being restored many times. One of these restorations was done by the member of the mayoralty, Knight Bryonianus Lollianus. The Sidetans let Ktistios know their gratitude on the base of the statue dedicated to him.

"The river reached the sacred city not only did it wish but you also tried hard and helped it. Ktistios, you brought it here

You repaired the water channels which currents destroyed by yourself,

You brought it here again,

Therefore, the Mayoralty of the district of Tetrapolits will suggest that a marble statue, which is more precious than gold, of yours to honour you.

God bless Ktistios

Ktistios: founder

Side's monumental fountain whose nine basins distributed water from the Manavgat River to the city.

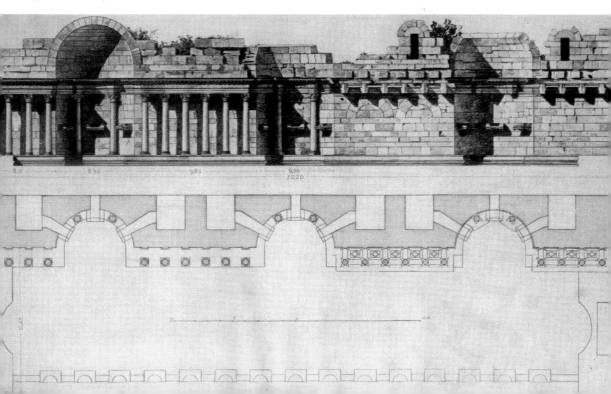

THE OYMAPINAR DAM

For the purpose of supplying electric power, this dam has been erected 75 km from Antalya, 20 km North of Manavgat.

The length of the lake is 5 km and water level 184 m. The elevation of the Dumanlı cave and exit of the underground river is 65 m. Oymapınar has the country's largest underground power station and it has been built entirely in the mountain. (nett fall:143m); power generated is 4x135=540 Mw and annual output is 1620x106 kwh.

The waterfall of Manavgat

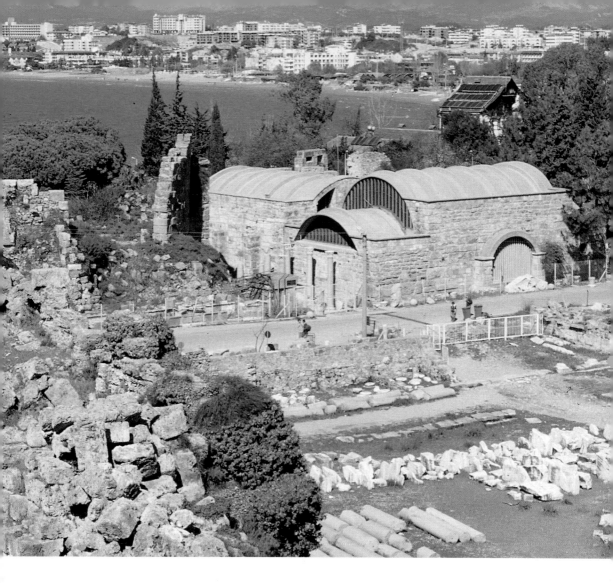

THE MUSEUM

The Side Museum is housed in a restored 5 th cent. A.D. baths complex, sited across the road from the agora. Access is by a narrow, colonnaded street, which led originally to the sea walls (walls of Philippus Attius). On the left of this street is a kiosk, where cold drinks, guide books, postcards, replicas, etc., may be purchased. The street continues to what was originally a courtyard, now a pleasant shaded garden, where sarcophagi, cinerary urns and fragments of Roman sculpture lie half-hidden among a profusion of flowering shrubs. Constructed during the last period of Side's prosperity, the building is rectangular in shape and follows the usual plan of a Roman bath. Restored through the initiative of Prof. Dr. A.Müfit Mansel from the İstanbul University who directed excavations at Side between 1947-67, it contains many of the antiquities discovered by him and his colleagues.

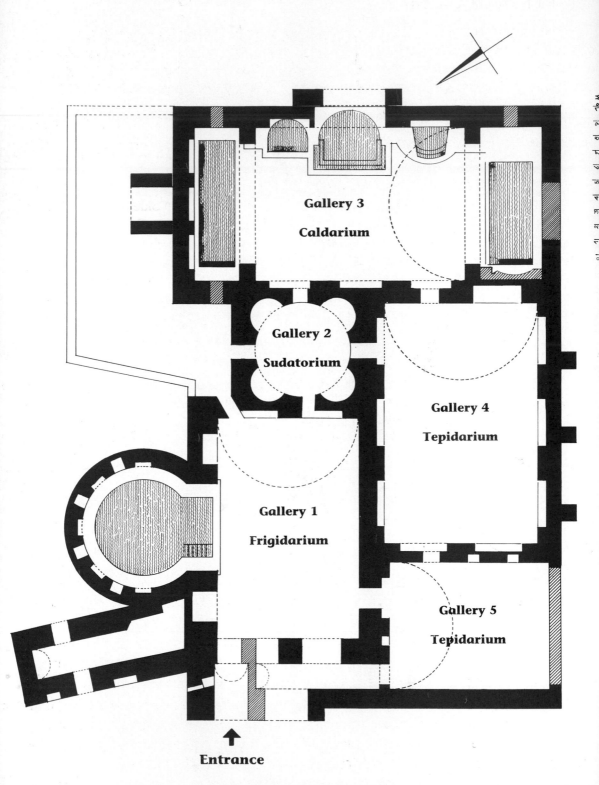

Entrance

Plan of the Museum

FRIGIDARIUM -GALLERY I :

The original entrance to the museum was by two arched doorways, which led from the courtyard to the frigidarium, the only unheated room in the baths. Originally roofed, the floor of this room is paved with re-used marble slabs, many bearing inscriptions. Its dominant feature is a large semicircular basin on the North-East, which was filled with cold water. Bathers descended into the basin- covered by a dome and lined with marble- by a flight of steps on the left. At the back, three niches which contained statues are set under four large rectangular alcoves. To the left of the basin is a narrow passage-way, through which water was conveyed from the aqueduct.

Along the wall facing the basin are the reliefs depicting arms, which were found at the city's East gate. These are believed to commemorate a victory by the Sidetans over an army from Pergamon in the 2 nd cent. B.C. In the centre of the room are two Roman altars, which were later hollowed out and turned into well-mouth. Between these altars a late Hittite column base, one of the oldest pieces found in Side to date, has been placed. Dating back to the 7 th cent. B.C. this basalt base was found near the Athena and Apollo Temples. This was adorned with a relief of branches intertwined with lotus flowers and buds. The sundial in the basin belongs to the Roman period, as do the fragments of the statues in the niches.

SUDATORIUM - GALLERY II:

A narrow doorway leads to the sudatorium, the hottest room in the baths, which was built over a furnace. Now circular in shape, it was originally square. The four niches in the corners contain a selection of small objects found in Side, excavations.

Reliefs from the East city - gate.

CALDARIUM-GALLERY III:

Continue into the caldarium, a rectangular room, which originally had basins at its North and South ends only. Later one large and two small basins were added on the East side. Facing the entrance is a beautifully-composed representation of the Three Graces. A favourite subject for artists, they were believed to symbolise beauty, friendship and gentleness. In the centre of the room is a statue of Hercules, holding the golden apples of the Hesperides. The niches above the basin to the left of the entrance contain Roman copies of Hellenistic statues of a woman and a girl. Along the side of the basin are a number of Roman amphorae, which were recovered from the Roman and Byzantian wrecks. To the left of the semicircular basins there is a relief of Ixion, King of Thessaly, who was condemned by Zeus to spend eternity bound to a rotating fiery wheel because of his attempted seduction of Hera. Nearby is a statue of the river-god, Melas (the modern Manavgat Çayı). In the niche of the right side basin is a relief of the birth of Aphrodite, which was found in the monumental fountain. A short 2 nd cent. B. C., inscription in the Sidetan language found near the East gate, is displayed near the central semicircular basin. In the basin at the South side of the room there are parts of a 2 cent. A.D. sarcophagus. The niche in the centre has a headless Nike, the goddess of victory, flanked by representations of Dionysos and Apollo.

Statues of a group of the three Graces (Charities) ➥

Statue of Hermes
(Hermes Centocelle)

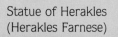
Statue of Herakles
(Herakles Farnese)

Head of Apollo
(Kassel Apollo)

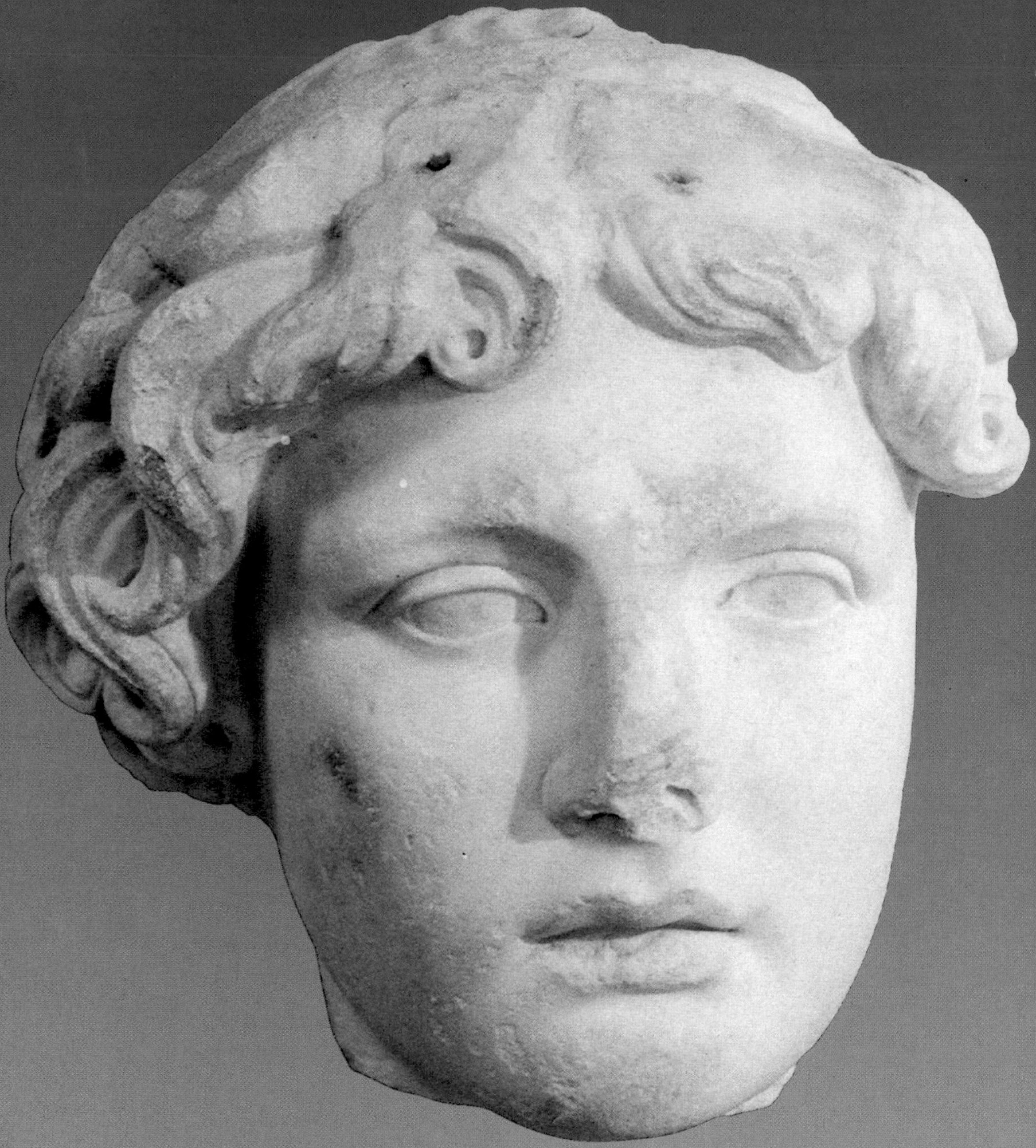

Head of Hermes
(Hermes Ludovisi)

Marble relief : The punishment of Ixion

TEPIDARIUM-GALLERY IV:

In the next room, the tepidarium, there is a headless statue of Nike, dated to the 2 nd cent. A.D., which was found in the library in the state agora. In a niche nearby there is a fine statue of Hygeia, the daughter of Asclepius, the god of healing. She has snake, twined around her arms, which came to be associated with the care and nursing of the sick. An almost complete statue of Apollo, dating from the 2 nd cent. A.D., is flanked by a head of Apollo and a head of Hermes. The head of Apollo is a Roman copy of the famous Hellenistic original known as the Kassel Apollo. The head of Hermes, who is depicted as a pouting, pensive youth, was discovered in the triple-basin nymphaeum near the museum. It was identified as a result of some interesting detective work. Archaeologist believe that in the 3 rd cent. A.D., when Side had become impoverished, a statue of Hermes was taken from another site in the city, suitably altered and in its new persona of Apollo re-erected in the nymphaeum. So far the body of this statue has not been found.

In the centre of the room, there is a Roman 2 nd cent. A.D. copy of the famous 5th cent. B.C. discus thrower and headless statues of Hermes and Ares, the god of war. Amongst other finds, Hermes was the guardian of merchants and so no doubt was very popular in a trading city like Side. A well-preserved statue of the god, also found in the area of the triple-basin fountain, stands in a corner of the room. He is show as a nude, muscular adolescent,

Sarcophagus of Eros

carrying a purse in his right hand. He is partly supported on his left by a herm: a plinth, which slopes gradually towards its base, decorated with a bearded head and phallus relief.

There follows a series of incomplete statues, dating from the Roman period. In a niche on the South side of the room are two 3 rd cent. A.D. sphinxes, which were found in the orchestra of the theatre. In the corner is a damaged statue of Demeter. An interesting composite statue of a Roman emperor is in a niche nearby. The head and torso belong to different periods. The body has been dated by the decoration on the armour to the 2 nd cent. A.D., while the head, which is much smaller in proportion, dates from the 4 th cent. A.D. As in the case of the Hermes head, it was changed in antiquity. The hair and beard were removed to create a new portrait.

Between two sarcophagi in the centre of the room, there is an altar, ornamented with two small male figures and bust. All date from the 2 nd cent. A.D. One sarcophagus, discovered in the East necropolis, is decorated with a frieze of children playing musical instruments and preparing for a sacrifice. On the back two griffin's face each other. On top there is a headless reclining male figure. The other sarcophagus, from the West necropolis, is ornamented on the sides with charming, tipsy erotes, who support each other in graceful couples. The cover of this sarcophagus is shaped like a roof. One pediment has a representation of Medusa, the other a round shield.

Torso of Nike. Found in 1954 in the Nymphaeum. Fine grained white marble.

Grave-stone of the captain from Side

Sarcophagus with Eros and garland decorations.

TEPIDARIUM-GALLERY-V:

The last room in the complex was probably the apodyterium. Now roofless, it provides the modern entrance to the museum. It contains a number of inscriptions from various monuments in Side and a giant, headless statue of Nike, which was found near the nymphaeum, which is sited at the principal gate to the city.

Amongst the most interesting finds in the garden are two fine sarcophagi. One has two erotes supporting a garland, with a column crater in the centre. On the other side there is an inscription inside a tabula-ansata. One of its pediments carries a damaged Medusa head. Along the wall there are some architectural fragments from a building near the necropolis. These show Selene, the moon goddess, and Helios, the sun god. Among the Corinthian and Ionic capitals, cinerary urns and fractured relief, there is an interesting triangular altar, with representations of a humped bull and a bay tree. This was found in the harbour area, near the temples of Apollo and Athena. A relief from the great baths, showing a procession of sea-creatures bearing gifts to the wedding of Poseidon and Amphitrite, is to be found by the wall on the North side of the garden.

A relief from the great baths. Nereides bearing gifts to the wedding of Poseidon and Aphrodite.

A relief of Medusa from the sarcophagus.

NOTES